STARTING

Over

STARTING

Over

*A Step-by-Step Guide
to Help You Rebuild Your
Life After a Breakup*

by Thomas A. Whiteman, Ph.D.
& Randy Petersen

PINON Press
P.O. Box 35007, Colorado Springs, CO 80935

OUR GUARANTEE TO YOU

We believe so strongly in the message of our books that we are making this quality guarantee to you. If for any reason you are disappointed with the content of this book, return the title page to us with your name and address and we will refund to you the list price of the book. To help us serve you better, please briefly describe why you were disappointed. Mail your refund request to: PiñonPress, P.O. Box 35002, Colorado Springs, CO 80935.

Library of Congress Catalog Card Number: 2001021283

ISBN 1-57683-236-8

Cover by Steve Eames
Creative Team: Brad Lewis, Lori Mitchell, Heather Nordyke

Some of the anecdotal illustrations in this book are true to life and are included with the permission of the persons involved. All other illustrations are composites of real situations, and any resemblance to people living or dead is coincidental.

Library of Congress Cataloging-in-Publication Data
Whiteman, Tom.
        Starting over : regaining me at the end of we / by Thomas Whiteman and Randy Petersen.
                p. cm.
            ISBN 1-57683-236-8
            1. Rejection (Psychology) 2. Separation (Psychology) 3. Loss (Psychology) I.
        Petersen, Randy. II. Title.
        BF575.R35 W47 2001
        155.9'3--dc21   2001021283

Printed in the United States of America

1 2 3 4 5 6 7 8 9 10 / 05 04 03 02 01

CONTENTS

INTRODUCTION

ReStart
Brianna's Story

"I never expected it to turn out like this."

Brianna's a doctor. For five years she was living with Craig, who worked for a pharmaceutical company. She envisioned marriage and children down the road, but they were both so busy . . . and so young. Then came Brianna's thirty-fifth birthday.

"Everything I dreamed for. Now it might be too late."

It was the normal mid-life panic of a childless single woman, except Brianna had a man, and a plan. "So, Craig," she asked, "have you thought any more about getting married and having children?"

"Um, well . . ."

Wrong answer, Craig. He was back-pedaling fast, the normal mid-relationship panic of a commitment-phobic male.

"Um, honestly, Bree, I kind of like what we have now. I'm not sure I want anything permanent. Isn't this what we wanted? No strings?"

The stringless wonder had been stringing her along for half a decade, while her biological clock kept ticking. Of course this birthday conversation became a huge fight. He packed his bags that night. Within a week he was out of her life.

"I had it all planned," she told her counselor. "I was going to work hard at my job, save up money, and have one child by the time I was thirty-six. Now that doesn't look possible."

She would soon be mourning the loss of Craig. You can't end a five-year relationship and not miss the guy, no matter how upset you are. But first she was focusing on her broken dreams: marriage, a child, PTA meetings.

"Do you know anything about artificial insemination? I could probably raise a child on my own, don't you think?"

She was grabbing for a quick fix—a way to get back what she'd lost. If she ended up rejecting single motherhood as an option, she'd be tempted to rush into a new relationship with a man she hardly knew. That would only cause more pain.

In fact there wasn't any easy answer for Brianna, no quick fix. She had to start over.

Adam's Story

"I'm sober for the first time in years. But I have no job and no relationship. I don't know where to turn."

Adam had just gotten out of a drug and alcohol rehabilitation center. He hadn't gone there willingly. Like many alcoholics, he hid his problem for many years, even from himself. But his marriage deteriorated with every drink. His work became shoddy. He went in with a hangover and left early for happy hour.

One day his wife walked out. That provoked a drunken binge that got him fired from his job. The following week he was arrested for driving under the influence. That's what eventually landed him in rehab.

"Where do I start?" he asked his counselor. "How do I put my life back together?"

Clean and sober now, Adam really had nothing to go back to. No wife, no job, only a very messy house with two mortgages. He clearly needed to start over.

Like Brianna, he was tempted to patch up his losses: get a job, jump into a new relationship. Now that he'd fought his way to sobriety, he should quickly be able to reassemble his life. But his counselor knew better. That's not "starting over," it's "picking up where you left off." You might be lucky enough to do that, but soon the old underlying problems will resurface.

It's like pulling weeds. You can clip them down, but they'll be back in a day or two. You need to root them out.

So Adam's counselor first got him connected to a chapter of Alcoholics Anonymous. Anyone triumphantly exiting rehab has to guard against relapse. But then it was time to dig into Adam's root issues. And his story was all too common. He had grown up in a wealthy but dysfunctional family. They had money but nothing else. Adam had always felt an emptiness. He drank to fill that void.

"Starting over" for Adam meant relearning a sense of self. He needed to think about who he was internally—what he liked, what he lacked, and what gave him satisfaction. He had to pay attention to his spiritual life, his emotions, his talents. What skills could he use in a new job? What qualities could he offer in a new relationship?

No Do-Overs

Computer games can be frustrating. You make one dumb mistake at level seventeen, and you have to start over. You'd love to come right back to the one screen you botched, but no—you have to go through sixteen levels to get back there.

Life can be like that too. You can't just patch up your mistakes. You have to take the time to rebuild. If Brianna grabs the first prospective father she meets, she's liable to suffer more heartbreak. If Adam rushes into a new job or relationship with no attention to his root problems, he'll be hitting the bottle again soon. They have to put their lives back together piece by piece. They have to rebuild from the bottom up.

Tom once counseled a teacher who had a tragic accident. Gloria's car was hit head-on and she went through the windshield, sustaining serious brain damage. She was only in her twenties, and she was lucky to be alive. As she came out of the coma, it became apparent that she had lost her language skills. She could speak a few words, but huge portions of her vocabulary were unavailable to her. She could look at a bowl of fruit and recognize the fruit, but she couldn't say, "Apple."

Gloria had to start from scratch, relearning the language like a toddler. Experts say it's even harder for adults to pick up lost language skills because children's brains are programmed to receive this new information and adults' brains aren't. But Gloria worked hard to regain her skills. Speaking. Reading. Writing.

Miraculously, two years after the accident, Gloria came back to her job, teaching special education at an inner-city school. "Working with these learning-disabled kids is completely different now, because I've been there," she said. "I have a whole new empathy for them."

Gloria's story can inspire anyone who needs a new start. You haven't suffered brain damage. But some sort of catastrophe has caused you *relationship* damage. You're wounded emotionally. You might be tempted, like Brianna or Adam, to patch up the problem and continue your life in stride. But the patch will tear. You need to start from scratch, as Gloria did, relearning the language of relationships.

It's not easy, becoming like a child again. You'll have to toss out some of your pride. Allow yourself to be a patient. Pamper yourself. Give yourself time to heal. Protect yourself from experiences that can reopen the old wounds. Chances are that you, like Gloria, will need a couple of years to heal from your wounds.

This book will challenge you to let the healing process run its course. It may frustrate you, even anger you at times, but its focus is on your rebuilding. We offer you eight ReStart Principles to help you understand how healing works. Within each chapter we also offer practical help to get through different stages of the healing process. These principles and guidelines have been developed through our observation of thousands of people struggling with broken relationships. As a professional counselor, Tom has worked with many such people, and he has gleaned much as a speaker and director with a divorce-recovery organization called Fresh Start. As a divorced man himself, Tom also knows this issue from the inside.

If you read this book when you're not in the midst of a divorce, you may observe that a lot of it seems like simple common sense: *Why did they say that? Doesn't everyone know how to deal with that situation or that kind of person?* Remember, if you're going through the recovery process, you simply may not be able to use your "common sense." In the midst of this stressful time, you're probably going to need help focusing on where you are in the recovery process, what you can expect next, and just how you'll get to that next step.

Similarly, if you read this book in a short time, you might find only a portion of it applies to where you are now. But keep it handy. In another few months, you might find a different part of it speaking to your needs. In fact, over the next two or three years, you might want to keep referring to it because you'll keep changing. You'll need different insights at different times along your personal path toward healing.

But here's the good news — the light at the end of the tunnel. As you let this process run its course, in the end you'll be a stronger person, better equipped to deal with life and better prepared for new relationships. You'll also have a new empathy for others in need, and you'll be uniquely capable of offering them help.

1

TAKING RESPONSIBILITY

> RESTART PRINCIPLE 1:
> *Miracles happen, but you must*
> *take responsibility for your own*
> *recovery.*

EVIE's husband had died four years earlier, but she was still deep in depression. She was referred to Tom for counseling, but he saw no improvement even after several months. He began to suspect there might be a "secondary gain" involved, meaning some benefit she might get from remaining troubled. Some people really don't want to start over.

So Tom asked her, "Is there anything good about your husband's death or your current situation as a widow?"

"What do you mean?" the woman replied.

"Do you gain anything by remaining depressed and complaining about how bad life is?"

This was an interesting angle for Evie—one she hadn't thought of before. "Well, people feel sorry for me. They try to help me. Some people cut my grass, and others help me financially."

Tom suspected that she was getting attention and support that she was afraid she'd lose if she became healthy again. "Evie," he asked, "do you really want to get better?"

She never answered the question verbally, but Tom was sure it struck home. In the following weeks and months Evie began to climb out of her self-pity. She got out more, joining a few church groups, buying some clothes, making new friends.

What was the secret of Evie's starting over? The simple answer is that she just had to want to. She had to take responsibility for her own recovery, instead of letting everyone else fret and stew over her. She had to decide *This is where I want to go and I'm going to get there.*

WHO'S RESPONSIBLE?

When he's not writing books, Randy spends some time directing plays at a local high school. The kids are great, but it's amazing to see how little responsibility they take for their own lives.

"I couldn't learn my lines because, like, I was going to last night, but then my dad decided to take us out to Dairy Queen and my little sister threw up."

"I missed rehearsal yesterday because I called Jeri for a ride and she never called back."

"I don't have my costume because my mom and me were going to go shopping last weekend but she had a meeting instead."

Part of the educational process is teaching these teenagers to stop looking for excuses and start looking for solutions: Study your lines on the school bus. Call someone else for a ride. Find a costume in your closet. Don't be satisfied to shrug and say, "Sorry, but there were circumstances beyond my control." *Take control* of the circumstances and do what has to get done!

This sort of behavior is understandable in teenagers, who are still dependent on their families. They're in that in-between stage where they're still learning how to fend for themselves. But the attitude carries over to many adults who somehow expect life to come to them. Look around at the twentysomethings you know and sort them out. Some are taking responsibility for their lives, some aren't. And over the next few years, with some of the currently non-responsible ones, you'll see the light come on, like that comic-strip bulb over the head. Plink! *I need to make something happen.* And they will.

After a painful romantic breakup, you're likely to feel victimized. Something bad has been done to you. You feel terrible *and it's not your fault!* Someone pushed you into this pit—why doesn't someone pull you out?

Let's be blunt—that's not going to happen. You're going to have to climb out.

Sure, there might be people around you to give you a boost. People might cut your grass or help you financially. But they can't do your starting over for you. That's your own responsibility. You have to take it.

Jay has to park his car on the street across from the apartment where he lives. Weeds have poked through the pavement in the crack between the street and the curb, right next to where Jay parks. At first Jay saw the weeds and said, "Hmmm, that's a bit unsightly. I'm sure the town will send someone to pull those up."

Over time the weeds grew. Now they were over the curb line. Jay figured that the owner of the service station on that side of the street would take care of it. After all, an untidy property would be bad for business.

The weeds kept growing. Now they were a foot high, and they scratched Jay's car as he drove up. He worried about the effect on his car's finish. Surely someone will notice this weedy patch and do something, he thought. But no one did.

Once, when the weeds were about two feet high, Jay had to load something into the passenger's side of his car—curbside. He had to brush aside the weeds in order to open the door, and when he closed it, some of the weeds were swept into the car. Now, besides the scratches on the outside, the weeds littered the inside of his vehicle. He became angry about the weeds, angry at the town, angry at the service station, angry at the weeds themselves. Someone should do something!

It was a constant source of irritation for him. Every day, as he went to his car, he grew angrier. No suburb-dweller should have to fight his way through a jungle to open a car door. *Why doesn't somebody take responsibility for this?*

And then his focus changed. It was that light-bulb-over-the-head moment. *Why don't I do something about this?* He borrowed some gardener's gloves and pulled up the weeds.

You might be doing the same thing as you recover from your breakup. Sure, you've been victimized by circumstances beyond your control. But stop waiting for someone else to do something. Put some gloves on and take control. Take responsibility for your own recovery.

MIRACLES

But don't miracles happen? Don't people find that, when they run out of their own strength, they rely on a higher power to get them through? In fact, some people would say that you have to realize you can't recover by yourself, and the harder you try the harder it gets.

We admit that miracles certainly occur. We've experienced

many moments in our own lives when we feel God stepped in to help us. Tom can point to several times in the recovery from his own divorce when he had to rely on God. Higher power? Absolutely.

But the problem is that some people treat their faith like a magic wand: Their prayers will undo all the damage. Certainly, God will make everything all right if they just have enough faith. We knew one woman who spent twelve years praying and trusting that her husband would come back to her. Janice kept setting a place for him at the dinner table and assuring her children that God would answer. This continued even after their father remarried and had other children.

We feel her faith would have been better spent in the grueling march toward accepting what had happened to her. If she had prayed for help in dealing with this crisis, she would have received some powerful answers.

Twelve years! That's an extreme case, but we find that many people take a similar approach, even if it's for a shorter term. And there are numerous advisers who will urge you: *Just have faith.*

Still Waiting

We do believe in miracles, and we know that sometimes people get the miracles they pray for. But we also caution against certain dangers of this approach.

It keeps you in denial. As we'll see in the next chapter, denial is the first stage of dealing with a tragedy. For a short time afterward, we don't quite grasp what happened, or we intentionally block it out. Maybe that's fine for a short time—a few months maybe. But extended denial is a problem. It keeps you from moving onward along the path toward acceptance and healing. In her conviction that God would definitely bring her husband back, Janice delayed her recovery for twelve years.

It ignores the natural ways God works. This is what we've observed. Sometimes God dazzles everyone with some supernatural miracle no one expects, but more often he seems to work within the natural order to answer prayers and help people. Humans have been created with a natural response to crisis, and we go through natural stages. That's a miracle in itself. It's irresponsible to insist that God overturn the natural process of healing in order to make you feel better instantly. That's imposing your own agenda on him.

It can focus on your own ability to believe, or your inability. At a certain point it stops being about God at all. Some people say that if you believe hard enough, or well enough, you can make those miracles happen. So when your prayers don't get answered, whose fault is it? Certainly not God's. You must not have enough faith, you loser! And so you end up feeling even worse about yourself because you lack the ability to summon God.

It can teach negative things about God. We worry about an approach that dictates to God what he must do. If he's truly a *Higher* Power, then maybe he should tell us how he's going to act. We also wonder about the backlash, say, with Janice's children. Instead of learning to trust in God's help for hard times, they're learning that God never gives you what you want.

If God isn't in your grid, then forgive our little side-trip into theology. We know that those issues are important for many people after divorce, bereavement, or a serious breakup. At the very time when they need their faith to help, they find it tripping them up.

We also recognize that many people find their faith during a crisis. As long as everything is going swimmingly, they don't need to think much about God. But when the world comes crashing in, suddenly they're asking God for all kinds of help. That's why Alcoholics Anonymous urges people to get in touch with their Higher Power. They're intentionally vague about naming it. They don't want to exclude anyone unnecessarily over religious sectarianism. But they've embraced the fact that we all need help along the path of recovery—superhuman help.

"You Gotta Help Me!"

So consider the generally non-religious man whose wife walks out, causing great pain and deep soul-searching. *This can't be happening. How could she? What did I do to deserve this? God, you gotta help me!* Suddenly, he is more aware of God than ever before.

Maybe he stops into a church or synagogue in town. Maybe he talks with a religious friend. Maybe his fervent sister-in-law starts giving him theology lessons. He doesn't know anything about God or the Bible, but he knows he needs help from some higher power. We just hope he gets steered in the right direction.

Well-meant advice like "Just believe" and "Pray for a miracle" and "Let go and let God" could cause a problem. They're not exactly wrong, just subject to abuse. It's that magic wand that he has to learn to wave. Personally, we have no doubts about the power of God, but we fear that this poor guy could get the wrong message about recovery, about God, about faith, and about himself.

Yet if that man, in his suffering and searching, wound up asking us for help, we'd tell him something like this: "God cares for you in your pain. We don't know why he let this tragedy happen; his ways are mysterious. But we know he'll help you deal with this.

Yes, he has the power to send some lightning bolt to make everything better instantly, but he seldom chooses to work that way. Yet he will work minor miracles in your life every day over the next few years as you come to grips with this crisis and rebuild your life. You'll go through some difficult times, but he'll never be far from you. You can trust in him for the strength to go through it."

Mad at God?

While crisis can often bring a person closer to God, it also drives some further away. It's common for people to cry out against God in anger. *Why did you let this happen? I don't deserve this suffering!*

At such times some people seem to lose their faith. Though they might have been very religious in the past, they stop their religious observance. It's as if they're trying to punish God for treating them badly. In some cases they also lose all interest in starting over. They could choose to go through the recovery process, but they'd rather sit and sulk. *God got me into this. Let him get me out.*

They're something like the little girl who's mad at her mother for not letting her go out to play before dinner. "Well then," the girl sniffs, "I'll just go to my room, and I'm not coming out." She stomps up the stairs in a huff.

Mom calls her for dinner, but she doesn't answer. Mom even knocks at her door, but the daughter is taking out her vengeance, punishing her mother by boycotting dinner. "All right, dear," Mom says, "we'll go on without you."

"Fine!" the child harrumphs through the closed door.

Then she hears the plink of tableware from the kitchen, along with the voices of her family. *I bet they'll be sorry that I'm not there.* But there's laughter from downstairs. They don't seem to be missing her at all. Then the girl begins to feel some pangs

Taking Responsibility 21

in her stomach. It sure would be nice to be eating with her family. She begins to realize that her hunger strike isn't hurting anyone but herself.

So the girl steps willfully down to the kitchen and announces, "I'm still upset. But can I have dinner?"

"Sure, honey," says Mom, pulling out a chair for her. "Maybe we can talk about it later."

Other books have explored all the philosophical and theological angles of being angry with God, so we don't need to get into that. Our concern is that you don't let your anger hinder your recovery. If you're trying to punish God by staying wounded, you won't hurt anyone but yourself. The victim thing gets old after a while. Sulking isn't going to get you where you need to be. The table is set for your healing. Come and join the family. You can talk about those anger issues later.

Working

Medieval monks had a saying: "God works and we work." We can apply that to the process of starting over after any sort of personal crisis. We all work through the stages of recovery, managing our anger, eventually reaching a point of acceptance and even forgiveness. But it's emotionally challenging to keep moving along that route.

By urging you to walk and work along that path, this book isn't denying that there's a Higher Power who will work with you. God works and we work. Any miracles that happen will occur along that path of recovery.

And the path of recovery is itself a kind of miracle. At several points in this book, we'll say, "Relax! Stop working so hard! Let the process happen!" Is that a contradiction? We don't think so.

God works and we work, *and the natural process works* to bring us back to health. Maybe it's like surfing, where you have to struggle to get to a certain place, but then you just ride the wave.

REAL LIFE STORIES
ABRAHAM LINCOLN & TOM

Abraham Lincoln

Many consider the sixteenth president of the United States to be the greatest of them all. Yet he grew up in what would today be considered extreme poverty, with uneducated parents who eked out a modest living by farming in Kentucky and later Indiana. Abraham's earliest memories were of farm chores, especially cutting wood. His mother, Nancy, died of "milk-sickness" when Abraham was 9, and his father remarried, primarily to have someone to keep house. But this stepmother awakened young Abraham's brilliant mind, teaching him to read, write, and "cipher," and piquing his interest in further learning. He began to borrow books wherever he could, but his main reading material was the Bible.

Abraham left the family around the age of 20 and held a variety of jobs, including ferryman, log splitter, postmaster, and clerk. He continued his efforts at self-improvement, reading Shakespeare and studying grammar with a local schoolmaster. Along the way he had a love affair with a woman named Mary Owens. We don't know much about this Mary—only that the breakup of this romance seemed to spur Abraham to rise above his lowly beginnings. Did she reject young Abe because he was "beneath her station"? Did she question his ability to provide for her? That's all conjecture; we only know he began to study law and was soon traveling the court circuit in Springfield. By this time he had earned the nickname "Honest Abe" for his earnest efforts to pay off some early debts.

In 1842, at the age of 33, Lincoln married Mary Todd, a well-educated, cultured woman. The two were of very different personality types, and it is recorded that Mrs. Lincoln was sometimes difficult to live with. Their marriage certainly had its share of sorrow. The couple had four children, but only one, Robert, lived to adulthood. Abraham is said to have borne his sorrows with patience and forgiveness.

Abraham ran for political office many times and was frequently defeated. But he never gave up, just as he never gave up on his marriage. From his lowly beginnings as a poor farmer's son to the presidency of the United States, he worked to make the most of himself, even when it seemed that life offered him insurmountable obstacles.

> *"The best thing about the future is that it comes only one day at a time."*
>
> —Abraham Lincoln

Tom

"Shame you couldn't get a real job."

The school janitor heard the snickering behind his back. Teenagers can be pretty cruel. All they saw was a man who had to mop floors for a living—probably a dropout, certainly a loser. The janitor wanted to tell them the whole story. He had a college degree. He'd been a professional. He'd bought a house. He'd been married.

But his wife had left him, and then the bottom dropped out. He lost his job. He lost his confidence. As he went through the emotional devastation of divorce, he had no drive. To pay the bills, he worked at a deli slicing meat—and here at the high school, mopping up after these smart aleck kids.

The janitor's name was Tom Whiteman. This is my story.

I spent a couple of years in a pit of depression and anger. My wife had ruined my life, I was convinced, robbing me of a promising future. I saw myself as a failure, a victim of circumstances beyond my control. After nursing my ill feelings for quite a while, I suddenly had a moment of clear thinking. "If you don't like your life," I told myself, "why don't you do something about it?"

Instead of blaming my ex, my fate, and God, I finally took responsibility for my life. How could I get out of my dead-end job? How could I start to rebuild? I decided to go back to school, getting a more marketable degree.

It wasn't easy, finding the right school, going through the application process, and then restarting my education—not to mention the financial crunch of paying school bills. I had to give myself a number of pep talks along the way. But I wasn't passing the buck anymore. I was taking responsibility for my own future.

In the following years, there were many events I can only call miraculous. So I don't think I can say that I "pulled myself up by my bootstraps." The power and love of God were very real to me, and without them, I wouldn't even have any boot-straps. But a key moment in my recovery was when I decided to stop moping and start coping. "If you don't like your life, why don't you do something about it?" Without that "Aha!" moment, I might still be mopping floors.

2

STAGE
FLIGHT

ReStart Principle 2:
The healing process involves stages.

Butterflies don't start off as gorgeous winged creatures. They begin as caterpillars, fuzzy worms that crawl around and eat dust. A stunning transformation occurs, turning some of earth's lowest beings into some of its highest. You probably knew that already.

But what you might have forgotten is that the transformation happens in stages. The fairy godmother of insects doesn't wave a wand and the caterpillar doesn't magically sprout wings. No, the little thing curls up, spins a cocoon, changes inside the cocoon, and then breaks out of it. For the butterfly to emerge, all those stages must be completed.

That's a fitting picture of recovery from divorce. After the initial breakup, you're eating dust. You feel like you're crawling through life. Then things start to change, and it usually seems that they're not changing for the better. Just as the caterpillar goes through a kind of death, wrapping itself in a coffin-like cocoon, in the same way a grieving person sinks deeper and deeper into depression. But that's not the end of it. Ultimately you can burst from your cocoon and fly free. However, you have to go through the stages.

LIFE'S A STAGE

Denial, Anger, Bargaining, Depression, Acceptance. We first began hearing that collection of terms about twenty-five years ago, as Elisabeth Kubler-Ross and others did research among the terminally ill and their loved ones. How did people deal with the loss of life? In these five predictable ways. It seems to be a pattern hardwired into the human psyche.

In our work with divorced people, we've seen the same pattern. Apparently, we deal with any loss this way, not just death. It's not always clockwork. Often, people slip back and forth among the stages. But people facing the breakup of their closest relationship regularly report feelings of denial followed by anger, bargaining, and depression. A healthy progression leads them to a point of acceptance, usually within a few years.

Sometimes people get stuck at a certain stage. If a man stops and spits whenever you say the name of the woman who left him ten years ago, chances are he's stuck in the Anger stage. If a woman is still on a diet five years after her ex told her she was too fat, she might be stuck in the Bargaining stage.

There's nothing wrong with being angry at your ex, or even being depressed about your divorce. You need to go through those stages. Just don't get stuck. That's a very important point—one that your well-meaning friends and relatives need to learn. When they start scolding you for being "in denial," ignore them. You need to deny for a while, then rant and rave, then try to figure out all sorts of odd ways to undo the damage. You're supposed to go through these stages. If you rush one of the stages, you'll just have to redo it later.

WHAT TO TELL YOUR FRIENDS

IF THEY SAY . . .	. . . YOU COULD RESPOND
1. It's been two months since (she) left. You ought to be over that by now!	1. The experts say it takes at least two years to recover from a breakup. It's like breaking a bone—if I don't take the time to heal properly now, it'll take a lot longer.
2. It's only a fling. [S]he'll be back.	2. If that happens, it'll be a pleasant surprise. But right now I need to accept the possibility that (s)he's gone for good.
3. Have I got the perfect person for you! [S]he'll make you forget all about the old one.	3. Thanks but no thanks. I'm not ready to begin a new relationship.
4. Stop being so angry. Anger doesn't do any good.	4. It's a stage I'm going through. I'll get over it.
5. Maybe (s)he'd come back if you lost 20 pounds.	5. If I lost 20 pounds, I might not want him/her back. Seriously, if the relationship is based on how I look, it isn't much of a relationship. If I lose weight, I'll do it for me. The relationship has weightier issues.
6. Still moping about your divorce? That was six months ago!	6. I know I'm depressed right now. But the experts say this is the last stage in my recovery. I'll be feeling better soon, but right now I need to grieve.
7. How can you forgive that [expletive deleted] after what [s]he did to you?	7. Forgiveness is more for me than for him/her. I know (s)he hurt me, but I need to let go of the grudge.

Stage One: DENIAL

Let's say you break your arm. What do you feel? Nothing. Oh, there's the initial pain of the break, and that can be excruciating, but soon thereafter your body rushes to protect you. The injured area begins to feel numb. In fact, you might even go into shock, as your body and mind conspire together to shut you down temporarily. You know you have an injury, and you're probably already rushing to the emergency room, so why should you have to keep feeling that terrible pain? Your body dulls your senses enough to get you through the worst of the pain.

Our emotions do the same sort of thing. We call it denial. After a traumatic emotional experience, we like to pretend it never happened. Or we seriously downplay its importance. "No problem. I can handle it."

Psychologists have tons of examples of people who just refuse to acknowledge the bad things that have happened to them. The widow who insists her husband is waiting in the car. The grieving parents who keep setting a place for their child at the dinner table. The accident victim who has blocked out the whole event. "Accident? What accident?"

Friends of people in denial often shake their heads in sympathy. "Poor Roger, he just can't take it." Denial seems unhealthy. After all, the person is unable to grasp reality. But denial is actually an important step toward health. As a temporary protection against overwhelming pain, denial (like physical numbness or shock) helps us heal.

- Sometimes people deny that a painful event happened at all.
- Sometimes people deny the magnitude of a painful event.
- Sometimes people deny their own role in the event.

The first kind of denial is usually short-lived, like the physical numbness that follows an injury. People might go a day or two, even a week, denying the entire trauma, but eventually it sinks in.

The second kind of denial is quite common, and it can last much longer. Even when people acknowledge that something bad happened to them, they can go years without accepting the full scope of the event.

The third kind is also common. It's a way of protecting oneself from adding insult to injury. If people are sensitive to guilt feelings, they might willfully ignore their own role in a tragic event. That way they won't have to feel guilt on top of the pain.

We often see denial in people recovering from divorce. Despite a host of warning signs, a man might refuse to believe his wife is having an affair. When she finally asks him for a divorce, he thinks it's just a phase she's going through. When she moves out, he tells himself she's just getting an apartment closer to her job. When he gets divorce papers, he figures her lawyer is just drumming up work.

Is he just a poor old sap? Maybe. But he's also going through a necessary stage. At first he's denying that anything's wrong. Eventually he realizes there's a problem, but he downplays its magnitude: "She'll be back. It's just her 'self-discovery' thing." If he ever realizes she's not coming back, he might still ignore the idea that his own neglect had any part in her actions. (We're not saying her infidelity is justified, just that his neglect might have contributed to it.)

If he recovers from this emotional trauma in a healthy way, he'll someday come to grips with the reality of the situation. He'll understand that she's gone for good and that she was very wrong to leave him, but he made mistakes too. He'll pass through denial into the other stages of recovery—anger, bargaining, and depression—and reach a point of acceptance and forgiveness, where he accepts reality and moves forward, learning from the experience and not holding grudges.

It's not bad to be in denial; like any other stage, it's bad to get stuck there.

In our experience with divorce recovery, six months is a reasonable period for denial. We're not holding a stopwatch to you, but if it's eight or nine months after the fact and you're still pretending that nothing serious happened, you're probably stuck in the denial stage. You might want to see a counselor to get unstuck. The duration will vary, depending on the timing and severity of the shock involved. In some cases the spouse just skips town suddenly with no warning. This kind of shock requires some major denial time. In most cases, though, the couple knows there are problems for months and even years before the ultimate breakup. The final split is still painful, but there's very little shock involved. Denial might last a day or two, and then people move right into anger.

Why do some people get stuck in denial? Here are a few reasons:

- They can't take the pain.
- They can't deal with the anger.
- They have no alternate vision of the future.
- They can't adjust their image of their ex-spouse.
- They can't adjust their image of themselves.

Actually, we humans deal pretty well with pain. We're wired to come through the numbness gradually and accept new pain in degrees, both physically and emotionally. Only the most over-protected souls need to stay in denial to avoid pain. It's more common for people to use denial to hide from their own anger. Many of us don't like feeling angry. When we feel that way we scare ourselves. Anger stirs up passions we would rather leave alone. Sometimes anger inspires hurtful actions. Often it destroys relationships.

In the wake of a marital separation or divorce, anger can be especially unpleasant. You've been wounded at the core of your being, and your ex is responsible. You want revenge. Yet this is a person you used to love. To rage against your ex is like raging against yourself, like tearing your own soul apart. Yes, those angry feelings are roiling within you, but you're afraid to give in to them. If you allow yourself to accept the full extent of your situation, there's no telling how angry you'll get. It's easier to keep a lid on your feelings, to stay stuck in denial.

Sometimes people keep denying a breakup because they honestly don't know any other way to live. They have no vision of the future that doesn't include their spouse. They still dream of growing old together, attending the kids' college graduations, traveling together to exotic locales. It's bad enough that your ex is on every page of your photo album, but he or she is in every glimpse of your future as well. If you accept the breakup, you'll have to write a whole new script for your life — and that can be daunting, especially when you're not feeling very confident. It's easier to deny things, to keep your dreams intact.

Some people idealize their partners so much that they can't imagine them doing anything wrong. "My husband wouldn't have an affair, I just know it." "My wife would never do anything to hurt me." And yet here's all this hurt in your heart, and your ex is halfway to Mexico with someone else. Facing reality would mean redefining the character of that person. And amid the shock and brewing anger, you're still very much in love. Maybe there's an explanation. There must be some good excuse. Outsiders wonder how some spouses can be so gullible, accepting flimsy excuses time after time, when obviously the partner is unfaithful. But those outsiders have never been on the inside of blind passion. People in love can practice a "willing suspension of disbelief" (to borrow a term from the theater), believing that the object of their affection can do no wrong. Even when faced with evidence to the contrary, it's easier to keep denying.

Sometimes people turn a blind eye to evidence of their own failings. This usually happens when they themselves initiate the breakup, but it can also happen when the other partner leaves. An unfaithful spouse can go to great lengths of denial to justify the infidelity. You see this regularly on the trashier talk shows these days (not that you would ever watch those): "Sure I cheated on you, because you were never there for me!" They deny personal responsibility.

But even when the other partner leaves, some people feel reluctant to view themselves in a new light. The loyal wife becomes a dumped divorcee. The good husband becomes a failure. To accept the breakup means redefining yourself as someone who couldn't keep the relationship together. You face that awkward moment with friends who innocently ask, "So where is . . . Bill?" "Give my love to Nancy . . . when you see her." You are no longer part of that familiar pairing. The two have become one, but not in the way you planned. In some religious circles, this redefinition is even worse. Officially or unofficially a stigma is attached to divorced people. You are deemed dangerous, unfit for service.

Recovery requires a certain redefinition of yourself. Eventually you must begin to see yourself as someone who has been through a difficult breakup, is growing through it, and will emerge stronger and wiser. But constructing a new self-image involves some heavy lifting. It's easier to stay in denial for a while.

Denial is the calm before the storm, a chance to catch your breath before the roller coaster ride begins. But the longer you stay in denial, the further out of touch with reality you become. Within a few months of your initial shock, you need to move forward, into the stages of anger, bargaining, and depression. Let the roller coaster begin.

Stage Two: ANGER
You're walking down the street minding your own business and suddenly someone slams into your shoulder. It's not a major injury, but still . . . your personal space has been violated. You're justifiably angry. You whirl around, ready to give your assailant a piece of your mind. "Do you mind? I'm walking here!"

Then you notice that the woman who slammed into you is on crutches, her leg in a cast. She's having some difficulty negotiating her way down the sidewalk. Stopping at your angry call, she turns and gives you a pitiful look. "Sorry," she murmurs. You nod your pardon and both of you turn to leave.

What happened to your anger? When your space was violated, you were ready to slug someone. Why didn't you? You could have grabbed that woman's crutches and thrown them in the street. But you saw that the woman couldn't help it. She wasn't trying to hurt you; she was just having some trouble with those crutches. She was a victim herself. And so you willingly swallowed your own victimization and gave her a break (so to speak).

This little overdramatized example teaches us several things about anger.

First, it's a natural, instinctive response. We don't usually decide to be angry. Anger bubbles up as a result of some bothersome event.

Second, while angry feelings arise instinctively, we can choose what to do about them. When jostled on the street, we might feel like slugging someone, but generally we don't.

Third, anger has to do with justice. What caused the anger in this story? The assumption that we were being mistreated. We have a right to walk down the street unmolested, and that right was being (almost literally) trampled on.

Fourth, anger rides on our perceptions, and those perceptions can change. What changed in this story? What melted the anger? Merely the changing perception. Is this some hoodlum brazenly bumping people on the street? No, it's a person struggling with a disability. We judge that woman "not guilty" of rudeness or neglect because she seems to be facing an injustice of her own.

We might define anger, then, as a natural response to a perceived injustice. And in the case of romantic breakups, injustice is often perceived. It's common for both parties to feel wronged when they split. "Why did you . . . ?" "If you hadn't . . . ?" "How could you . . . ?" Blame flies furiously.

But even when it's hard to fix blame for specific deeds, we still feel anger churning within. There's a kind of "anger logic" that takes over. It goes something like this.

- I feel awful.
- I don't deserve to feel awful.
- I feel awful because of you.
- You have made me feel this way, which I don't deserve.
- I am angry at you.

Anger is odd that way. As you can see, it's actually not very good at logic. Anger doesn't focus very well on specific reasons or even specific people. When you're angry, you lash out. One driver swerves dangerously in front of you and speeds off, and you're likely to curse out the next driver who passes you.

Anger is a fire. Actually, this is a very good image because fire is both good and bad. Where would we be without it? Still in caves munching raw dinosaur, no doubt. Fire warms us, cooks our food, lights our way, and inspires songs like "Kum Ba Yah." But fire can also burn down our homes.

Not long ago a forest fire raged through New Mexico, burning many trees and a number of homes, and threatening a nuclear reactor. The irony was: this fire was purposely set . . . by the Forest Service. It was supposed to be a "controlled burn," thinning out one section of the forest so new vegetation could develop there. But high winds and dry, hot conditions drove the fire out of control, and it became a disaster.

Anger is like that. As you come out of denial, you feel the anger start to burn. That's a good thing. You've got a lot of "perceived injustice" to burn off to make way for new vegetation. Allow that "controlled burn" to happen, but keep watch. Don't let it rage out of control. It's liable to flare out at the wrong people, and it might lead you into dangerous actions.

Learning from Anger
So let's get back to our definition of anger as a natural response to a perceived injustice. What can we learn from this about the anger stage of recovery from a breakup?

1. Let yourself feel the anger. Some might think this is absurd to say. They feel anger very easily—maybe too easily. But others have always been taught to keep a lid on their angry feelings. It's not "nice" to be angry. It's not "righteous." It's not "civilized." Well, forget all that. If you feel wronged after a breakup, you'll feel angry. This is a natural response. It doesn't do any good to try not to feel angry. It's unnatural. The feelings are there; you have to do something with them. Medical literature is full of the effects of bottled-up anger. If you don't let your anger come out in normal ways, it will come out in some other, probably unhealthy, ways. Ulcers, high blood pressure, and back strain are just a few of the physical symptoms. The psychological and spiritual results can be just as debilitating.

2. Express your anger in thorough, but healthy ways. You don't have a lot of control over the angry feelings that arise inside you. They are, as we've said, a natural response. (You might gain some control by learning to perceive things differently, but more on that later.) Yet you have great control over how you choose to express your angry feelings. Yes, there are some people with notoriously bad tempers who seem to lose control when they're riled. We feel that even these people can learn to control their actions, though it takes some discipline. But for most of us, it's not that difficult.

We've noted with some amusement the changing policy of *The Jerry Springer Show*. Not that we ever watch that show, mind you, but it used to be that angry guests would throw chairs around. Then someone decided it was too violent (and perhaps too vulnerable to lawsuits), so they stopped throwing chairs. The guests are just as angry, but now they don't throw chairs. Why? Because they're not allowed to. Because burly guys in black shirts will jump up and stop them. But if they're truly out of control, why would that matter? In their fits of anger, they must be choosing whether to throw chairs or not. That example might be a bit too theatrical. We trust the talk shows about as much as we trust pro wrestling, and sometimes it's tough to tell them apart. But still the point remains: We generally choose our angry behavior. Our feelings propel us into actions we wouldn't normally do, but we can still choose to refrain from certain actions, no matter how mad we are.

However, anger will come out in some way. When you start to feel angry, you begin a chain of physical and emotional events that have to run their course. You tense up, your heart beats faster, your body gets primed for a fight. Even if you keep yourself from doing something harmful, that energy has to go somewhere. Bottle it up, and you'll get an ulcer or worse. Let it fly, and you're liable to hurt yourself or innocent bystanders. (Athletes get more injuries from fights with water coolers than with other players.) The secret is to channel your angry energy in good ways. Run a mile. Write a song. Paint your house.

3. Keep justice as your goal. If anger is ultimately about justice, then we should be seeking justice even when we're angry. Unfortunately, once the blood starts to boil, it's easy to lose sight of the ultimate goal.

Let's say your ex has treated you badly. You're understandably angry. Why? Because it's not fair. You've given that person the best years of your life and this is the thanks you get? Now you want your ex to suffer. You get the best lawyer you can and you try to squeeze every last penny out of the settlement, whether you need it or not—simply because you want to hurt this person who has hurt you. That'll even things up. It will seem like justice.

But here's the biggest problem with anger. It appropriately starts by seeking justice, but soon gets high on revenge. You begin by aiming for "an eye for an eye," but soon you're blasting the person's whole head off. Anger goes overboard, and soon you're treating the other person unjustly, so he or she tries to "get even" with you, but goes too far, making you even angrier . . . and soon you're fighting a world war.

So be careful about expressing your anger. It's important to go through the anger stage, being completely honest about your feelings of rage. You might even do some things to try to "settle the score," but keep an eye on justice. Don't let your anger create a worse situation.

4. When things cool down, check your perceptions. Perhaps the most important word in our definition of anger is "perceived." We respond angrily to situations that seem unjust to us. When we think we're being mistreated, we lash out. Remember the story about the woman on crutches bumping you on the sidewalk? You start to become angry when you think she's being irresponsible. But once you get the full picture, you ease up.

Learn to look at the situation through the other person's eyes. Let yourself role-play the scene in the opposite role. How does that person view you? What seems fair to him or her? This is a crucial skill in business negotiations and politics. It's just as crucial in personal relationships.

Many conflicts are just matters of misunderstandings. Two people want different things but assume they want the same thing. You think the other person is trying to hurt you, when he or she is actually clueless about your feelings. Or you expect others to share your priorities when they don't. If you learn to get behind the eyes of others, to think as they think, you'll avoid many of these misunderstandings.

There will still be times when you get hurt, unjustly. Your anger will boil over because of how you've been mistreated. But even then, your broader perception will help you know exactly what the issues are, and it might help you channel your anger better.

Dealing with Anger

There are four basic ways you can deal with anger:

1. Rage. A fire burns within you, and you let it burn out of control. You scream, hit, and hurt in any way you can. Sometimes an angry outburst can seem to be satisfying, to "get it out of my system." But it can be dangerous, too. And your anger can spawn other anger in yourself or in others, and the conflict escalates.

2. Repress. You remain "in control," stuffing your anger deep within you. On the surface, your relationships seem polite and peaceful. But you're a volcano inside. That fire may seep out in bitterness, sabotaged relationships, or personal stress. Some counselors will tell you it's healthier to rage. We recommend that you move forward, to redirection and resolution.

3. Redirect. Tom couldn't sleep, he was so angry over his divorce. So one day he decided to redirect that angry energy in a positive direction. He remodeled his basement. At 3 A.M. he'd be pounding nails or laying tile. This had several positive effects. (1) It kept him from doing something nasty with that anger. (2) It wore him out so he could sleep better. (3) It got him a new basement. Look for some project of your own, where you can invest your fiery energy. But be careful about throwing your passion into a new relationship—it's likely to burn hot and fizzle quickly, causing even more damage.

4. Resolve. This is where you're headed eventually. If you're like most people, you can't get to a resolution point for a year or two after the anger stage begins. But remember that you're going in that direction. Ultimately, your anger can fade as you forgive and accept and move on.

Stage Three: BARGAINING

"If you come back to me, I promise I'll never yell at you again."

"If I could lose twenty pounds, I know he'd come back."

"God, I'll serve you all my life if you just bring her back to me."

Bargaining is the most complicated stage of recovery from a breakup. It's akin to denial because you think you can undo the damage if you only do a certain thing. But usually the damage is far too great for your quick fixes. Yet bargaining is a step forward from anger. At least now you're thinking about ways to make peace. And bargaining represents that last grasp of hope before you tumble into despair. Ultimately you'll realize that, yes, it's really over—forever finished and done with. But when you're bargaining you still think there's a chance.

A friend of ours likes to say that bargainers try to apply microwave solutions to crockpot problems. In other words, your breakup took years to simmer into reality; you're not going to zap it away with some momentary impulse. If your relationship has been steadily eroding away, restoration will take more than a makeover, a vacation together, or a trip to the shrink.

You might think that bargaining is a fairly benign stage, without the dangers of anger or the pains of depression, but there are still a couple things to watch out for.

Don't sell yourself short. Some people get so desperate that they'll promise anything for one more shot at the relationship. We knew one guy who offered to let his wife continue her affair if she would just move back home. Keep your dignity. Observe proper boundaries. Manipulative mates can play this stage to their advantage, especially if you're negotiating divorce settlements or custody arrangements. Make sure you stand up for what you know is right and appropriate.

Don't set yourself up for a fall. Sure, there's something inevitable about bargaining. You're going to make a last-ditch effort to restore things. You're going to get your hopes up, and you're going to be disappointed. Then you'll have a time of depression. Isn't that a cheery outlook? So we're not saying, "Don't bargain." It's part of the natural progression of stages. Just be careful about it. Don't take outlandish risks, physically, financially, or emotionally. The higher your hopes in this stage, the deeper your depression in the next.

In some cases, bargaining "works." Loretta had been telling Mark about her problems with the marriage, but he wouldn't listen. Then she moved out. Mark was stunned at first, dismissing it as a passing fancy, then becoming angry. Loretta kept in contact, however, and eventually Mark reached the point where he asked, "What do I have to do to get you back?" That's when the bargaining started. After a few months of regular discussion, Loretta moved back in with Mark. Their issues weren't all resolved, but Loretta saw enough positive changes in Mark to give their marriage another chance. Mark was wounded by this whole ordeal, but he was willing to try again.

Sadly, that's the exception rather than the rule. In this case, Loretta still wanted to be married, and she just moved out to force Mark to pay attention to her issues. Not all spouses who move out are that committed to the relationship. When bargaining works, it's because both parties work together. Progress isn't made through drastic changes, but by steady, slow commitments. Wild promises will not woo your partner back to you; they will only cheapen you.

Stage Four: DEPRESSION

Emotionally speaking, depression is an empty tank. You've grasped at the hopes and raged at injustice and suffered the pains of loss, and now you just close up. You're not just sad; you're swimming in a sea of sadness. Actually, swimming would be too much effort. You are floating in that sea—maybe sinking. You have no energy. You have no hope.

Physical symptoms of depression include sleep disturbance, changed eating patterns (too much or too little), irritability, exhaustion, and susceptibility to illness. It seems like your body is falling apart, just like the rest of your life.

People will try to talk you out of depression. "Cheer up. Things can't be that bad. Turn that frown upside down." They mean well, but they just don't get it. Depression is something you need to go through. You can't paste a smiley face on it and pretend it's not there. You've suffered a major loss in your life, and you need to grieve for it. So, for a time, you'll be too sad to get up in the morning. You'll probably trudge through your workplace not really caring what gets done. Most likely, you'll be hard to live with.

We need this depression to convince us that the relationship is finally over. There's a logic to these recovery stages. First we deny that there's a problem, or at least a serious problem, then we get mad at the other person as we begin to feel the pain. Bargaining is a lurch back toward denial as we try to make things all better. As long as we're bargaining, we never quite grasp the finality of our loss. But as those false hopes of the bargaining period fade, we sink into depression.

As with the other stages, problems occur when you stay too long in depression. People often remain depressed for about a year, but if you're facing your second springtime in the throes of depression, it's time to take a walk and breathe some fresh air. Honestly, many folks just seem to snap out of their depression one day as they realize they don't need to mourn anymore.

But you can't rush this stage either. If you try to snap out of depression before you're ready, it won't last. But when you're ready, you need to take the risk of living again. Allow yourself to enjoy yourself.

Problems also occur when depression drags people deeper than they should go. If you're suicidal, or if your lethargy is seriously affecting your work life or your family life, get professional help. Medications are available to fight the more serious symptoms of depression. Of course, some people in deep depression try "self-medication," drinking heavily, taking illegal drugs, or overdoing prescription meds. This is dangerous, and it tends to make the depression worse. People with addictive personalities might also turn to addictive behaviors as an escape from their depression—gambling, pornography, overeating, shopping, or shoplifting. These might offer a temporary way to forget your problems, but they almost always make your situation worse.

Our suggestions for getting through the depression stage?

1. *Enjoy your sad mood for a while.* Don't feel guilty for feeling sad. You need to go through this.

2. *Let your loved ones know you need to grieve for a year or so.* Don't let them send you on a guilt trip. Beg their indulgence. But be careful not to be too surly toward those who care the most about you. You need them.

3. *Watch out for addictive behavior.* You know your greatest temptations, so guard against them. Ask your closest family members or friends to hold you accountable.

4. *Monitor yourself for serious problems and be ready to get help.* If you're suicidal, unable to go through the basic functions of life, or are getting into some addictions, call a counselor. (In fact, plan in advance what counselor you'll see if things get bad. Have the number at hand. Later, when you need to make the call, you might not even have the energy to use a phone book.)

Stage Five: ACCEPTANCE

That that is is that that is not is not is not that it it is.

You've just read the secret of stage five, acceptance. Huh? First, let's punctuate that sentence.

That that is, is. That that is not, is not. Is not that it? It is!

Acceptance is simply a matter of seeing the situation "that is." You stop grabbing backward for some past relationship "that is not." You're finally able to convince yourself that you're living in the present, free from the past, and you need to step forward into the future. Is not that it?

It is!

You don't have to do much. Some people go through their recovery like a "to do" list, checking off stage by stage. Books like this are quick to offer tips—ways to keep moving along. But the acceptance stage defies all attempts to pin it down to pointers. It's just seeing what's there, as well as stopping the evasions of stages one to four.

In acceptance, you've stopped denying the loss of this relationship. You know it's over.

In acceptance, you stop boiling in anger against the other person, against yourself, against others, or against God. Perhaps you realize that continuing anger does nothing to create justice; it just hurts you more.

In acceptance, you stop searching for quick fixes, bargains, and ways to go back in time. "If only I did . . ." "If only I could . . ."

You realize the irrelevance of these hypotheticals.

In acceptance, you finally climb out of the depression that has imprisoned you. You've finished your time of mourning and you're ready to greet a new day. You might still entertain a wistful thought or choke back an occasional tear, but you recognize that good things await you in the future. No need to stay chained to the past.

Acceptance means moving on. You don't have to say that your suffering was all right. Some people learn to say that they grew through the process, but you don't have to. Your breakup and the following slide into depression might remain a black hole in your life, something you'd rather not think about. You don't have to accept that it was good, just accept that it happened as a normal part of the recovery process and that you've lived to tell about it.

Acceptance means assimilating the experience into your life. It means understanding that the experience has changed you, that you are a somewhat different person. Not better, not worse, just different. It might be like that tough computer course you took at the community college, or like that peanut butter you spooned out of the jar yesterday. For good or ill, it's now a part of you. The knowledge in your head, the fat cells on your hips, or the scars on your soul—you now go through life as a changed person. In the acceptance stage, you stop denying that, fighting it, or bemoaning it; you just realize it.

Acceptance means letting go of the pain. As we just said, it doesn't mean forgetting about what happened, but it does mean refusing to let the pain of the past dominate your life in the future. Some people are actually reluctant to step forward into the acceptance stage because they've learned to like their pain. They've been nursing their wounds in their own private depression, and perhaps they've gained pity from others. They've allowed their pain to define who they are. Joe becomes "Poor Joe . . . you know his wife left him." Carol becomes "Poor Carol . . . she just fell in love with the wrong guy." Pain can become so ingrained in your life that you can't imagine any other way to live.

There's a wise analogy from Africa about a monkey trap that merely consists of a banana in a jar. A monkey can reach into the jar and grab the banana, but the jar's opening is too small for it to pull its hand out while holding the banana. Apparently, monkeys will go around for hours with that jar on their hands, unwilling to let go of the banana. People do the same thing, clinging to the problems they say they want to get rid of. They simply don't think they can let go.

But that's often the solution to our suffering—merely letting go of it. Monkeys eventually get tired and give up the banana. The jar comes off, and the monkey is free to swing the trees in search of other bananas. Similarly, the acceptance stage usually comes when people get tired of holding on to their pain. They let go, and they start living life again.

Stage Six: FORGIVENESS

Most recovery systems end with acceptance, but in our dealings with victims of shattered relationships, we've realized that a sixth stage should be added. Perhaps if you're dealing with death or disease (the subjects of early research into stages of recovery), the five stages will suffice, but a broken relationship requires some sort of resolution for the relationship.

Don't get scared away by this. It doesn't mean that the relationship gets put back together. It doesn't necessarily mean that the two former partners become friends again. But it does mean that they learn to release their animosity, and they eventually define a new relationship with healthy patterns and effective boundaries.

We devote a whole chapter to this later, so we'll just touch on a few details here.

Three key questions will determine the nature of the forgiveness you offer.

1. How one-sided was the problem? Were you a rather innocent victim in the breakup, were you the villain, or were you both pretty nasty? This will determine whether you need to ask forgiveness as well as offer it.

2. Does the other person want to be forgiven? If so, then you can talk about the problems that occurred and ultimately let go of your resentment. If not, you can still "forgive" unilaterally—meaning that you refuse to let a grudge poison your own soul.

3. Is there an ongoing relationship of any kind? If you share custody of children, you'll have to find a kind of coexistence with the person who broke your heart. Forgiveness can get you there. If you know you'll see your ex around town, forgiveness can shield you from new wounds.

Many people carry the misconception that forgiveness involves making excuses for the offender. "That's okay." "No problem." "Don't worry about it." But the truth is exactly the opposite. When you forgive someone, you're saying that there is a problem that has to be dealt with. The other person did something wrong. Otherwise there'd be nothing to forgive. The forgiver says, "You wronged me, but I will not hate you for it."

The offender may choose to accept your forgiveness or not—

or might be starting a new life in Rio. That doesn't matter. As we noted above, if you hold a grudge, you'll only pollute your soul. When you offer forgiveness, you're doing deep cleaning.

REAL LIFE STORIES
→ KING DAVID & MARK

King David

At first reading, the biblical story of David and Bathsheba seems to be a fairly straightforward tale of a powerful man who used that power to take advantage of those around him. David was king of Israel. Though renowned as a warrior, on this occasion he stayed home in his palace as his troops fought on some distant front. Strolling on his rooftop, he spied a beautiful woman bathing on another rooftop. When he found out her husband was off at war, he slept with her. As it turned out, she became pregnant.

Most kings of that era could take any woman they wanted and get away with it, but Israel was ruled by divine law. Bathsheba's pregnancy would cause a major scandal. Adultery in the palace! And how would David's troops feel when they learned that the king had committed adultery with the wife of one of their fellow soldiers?

So the king hatched an ingenious cover-up plan: Bring her husband back from the front to reward him for a job well done. He would sleep with Bathsheba and think that the child was his own. Crisis averted! But the husband refused to bed his wife while his comrades suffered on the front lines. Instead, he slept outside the palace.

That's when the story turns uglier. David sent the husband back to battle carrying a secret message to the general: Put this guy on the front lines and then withdraw without him. The order was followed. The man was killed in battle. In a phony show of sympathy, the king magnanimously asked the grieving widow Bathsheba to be his own wife. What a guy!

With a new wife and soon a new baby, David thought the threat of scandal was behind him. But then the prophet Nathan showed up, telling a story about a rich man who stole a poor man's only lamb and then had the lamb killed. "How dare he!" thundered the king. "Who is that man? I'll see that justice is swiftly enacted!"

"You are that man," said Nathan.

The king had been successfully denying the problem. It took a simple story to jolt him out of denial. Then he plunged into a maelstrom of anger, guilt, bargaining, and depression. (He wrote about his feelings in Psalm 51.) The child of his adulterous union became very ill, and the prophet announced that this was God's judgment. David began bargaining with God for the life of this child. Then, realizing his guilt, David became depressed, refusing to eat, sleeping on the ground, and constantly praying.

When the child finally died, David's servants were afraid to tell him out of fear that he would do something desperate. But when he heard the news, David got up, bathed, changed his clothes, ate a hearty meal, and comforted Bathsheba. This is a classic example of the suddenness of acceptance. Often a person simply reaches the end of the grieving process and gets up and lives normally again.

As Psalm 51 makes clear, forgiveness was also a major issue here—not that David needed to forgive anyone, but he sought forgiveness from God, and got it.

Obviously, David's story isn't about a divorce or romantic breakup, but we do see the classic stages associated with a traumatic life-change: denial, anger, bargaining, depression, acceptance, and forgiveness.

We also get some insight into the emotional processes of a person who has brought on his own misfortune. Many of those who are "starting over" after a failed relationship have been victimized, but others are the victimizers. They've made major mistakes that have doomed their relationships, and now they're afflicted not only by the pain of the lost union, but also by guilt. David knew that feeling. "For I know my transgressions," he prayed, "and my sin is always before me" (Psalm 51:3, NIV).

As an interesting postlude to David's story, he remained married to Bathsheba and eventually they had another son named Solomon. This son grew up to be the greatest king of his time in the Middle East and probably Israel's most powerful king ever.

> *"Let me hear joy and gladness; let the bones you have crushed rejoice. . . . And grant me a willing spirit, to sustain me."*
>
> —King David

Mark

Working as a counselor, Mark knew the stages of recovery by heart. He'd coached many people from denial to acceptance.

So when his wife announced that she was going to leave him, he knew the drill. Of course, that didn't change anything. He went through all the stages just the same.

Knowing that a divorce might affect his work and decrease his income, Mark's wife gave him six months' notice. That just created a surreal period when Mark started going through the stages privately, without any public awareness of his plight.

First came denial. *She can't be serious. We can work this out. After all, she's still living here. We're just going through a bad time.* But she was serious.

As Mark realized that, he became angry. *Why is she doing this? What did I do to deserve this?*

Once he got that out of his system, he began bargaining. "How can we fix this? Do I need to change? Tell me what you need from me, honey, just don't leave!"

But she left six months after her private announcement to Mark. That plunged him into a deep depression. You might think that her way of easing him into divorce would lessen the severity of the crisis. Instead, it might have made it worse. And you might think that his familiarity with the stages would have kept them from bothering him. Nope. He simply knew what was coming. Depression didn't creep up on him, but it hit him hard—it cost him his job. He was far too troubled to listen to anyone else's problems. He began working at a camp, where he could help people in physical and organizational ways without counseling them.

After about a year of depression, he attended a seminar that Tom Whiteman was leading. As Tom talked through the stages, Mark was nodding vigorously. Not only did he know these stages from his psych textbooks, but now he knew them from his own life. He was a poster child for the stages of recovery.

Shortly afterward, Mark began to feel better. Not that Tom's seminar was any wonder cure—the depression had simply run its course. Mark started looking for ways to use his counseling ability again, so he could share not only his expertise, but also his experience.

3

TIME
TUNNEL

RESTART PRINCIPLE 3:
Healing takes time.

KEITH had that frustrated look in his eyes—the one that says,
"I'm sick and tired of being sick and tired." It had been less than
a year since his wife had announced she was leaving him. She had
tried to be nice about it, as nice as one can be when walking out
on a seven-year marriage. That only made it worse. How's a guy
supposed to feel when the love of his life says, "Honey, I still like
you, but I need more"?

Suddenly she was gone, and he was left picking up the pieces
of his shattered self-image. Some days, at work, he could almost
pretend that she would be waiting for him at home. But the
empty house kept reminding him of the stark truth. Other days
he would get angry at her. It wasn't easy at first. Her vanishing
act had all the charm of Glenda the Good Witch, implying that
she was just following her bliss and he was sadly inadequate. But
Keith managed to break through that facade and rage against her.
No matter how sweet she was, she had still reneged on her marital promises.

In the short time since her departure, Keith had toyed with

the bargaining stage. His prayers were full of exorbitant vows—if only God would bring her back. There were even a few phone calls with her, and he searched for some way to woo her back.

But Keith sank pretty quickly into depression. His health suffered. Back pain, exhaustion, stomach problems, he put on weight. He found it hard to drag himself to work; sometimes he didn't. At night he'd bury himself in the easy chair in front of the TV. He had a few friends who loyally checked up on him, trying to get him up and around, but what could they do? He had zero energy.

From this pit of depression, he looked at his friend with that sick-and-tired expression and said, "It's been almost a year now. I should be over this."

Keith was compounding his problem. Not only was he thoroughly, classically, clinically depressed, but now he was also worried that something worse was wrong with him. In the words of that old commercial, "I've fallen and I can't get up!" He was afraid that his temporary woes would be permanent. Would he ever enjoy the light of life again?

Fortunately, his friend knew better. "It usually takes at least two years to recover from a divorce," he replied, "sometimes longer, up to five years in some cases."

That was good news and bad news for Keith. He certainly didn't relish the thought that he'd probably be staying in this pit of depression for another year or more, but he was actually encouraged by the news that he was normal. This wasn't some mysterious, languishing problem. He was moving right along a timetable of recovery. In fact, Keith thanked his friend profusely for that information. He was still depressed, but now he was less worried.

That conversation occurred several years ago, and Keith has since come out of his depression, following the timetable rather precisely. At around the two-year point, he began to step out from his "cave." He still did some sulking, but he began to get out more. He became more reliable at work. At around the three-year point, he joined a group of friends who shared a love of film. They went to movies and spent hours discussing them afterward. At around the four-year point, he began exercising regularly, to take off some of the "divorce weight" he'd gained.

RECOVERY TIMETABLE

In the last chapter, we talked about how the acceptance stage often begins literally overnight. You wake up and smell the coffee—and you drink the coffee and you re-enter life. Sometimes it happens the way it did with Keith: a slow emergence from the pit of depression. Sometimes you have to take those baby steps to get walking again.

In the world of professional sports, if a player breaks a leg or tears a tendon, team doctors quickly announce how long they expect recovery to take. The quarterback is out for the season. The pitcher gets put on the "15-day disabled list." The power forward is expected back for the second round of the playoffs.

How do they know these things? Well, they know how the human body works. It heals at a certain pace. There's a range, of course. Some people heal more quickly than others. That power forward might surprise everyone by coming back for the first round of the playoffs. The pitcher might have to be moved to the 30-day disabled list. But, within a certain margin of error, we expect certain injuries to heal in a certain amount of time.

The same thing is true of human emotions, though we don't

often hear about it. People routinely heal from divorce within two to three years, although some take longer. People recover from the death of a spouse within a year or two. If the "break" is not so bad, it might heal more quickly. That torrid three-week romance will cause you grief when it fizzles, but it shouldn't set you back for more than a month. On the other hand, you might take longer to heal from divorce or bereavement if there are extenuating circumstances. If your ex and the new lover move next door to you, that will probably prolong your recovery. If the loss of your spouse was sudden, you will probably take longer to work through the early stages of recovery, especially denial.

These are the major factors that determine how long your recovery will take:

- Length of relationship
- Depth of commitment
- Intertwining of lives
- Shock of loss
- Possibility of renewed relationship
- Reopening of wounds
- Quality of recovery
- Support network

Length of relationship. How long were you together? In general, the breakup of a short-term relationship will be easier to bounce back from. Over time, two people meld their lives together, so it becomes more and more painful to tear them apart.

Depth of commitment. Broken marriages take longer to recover from than dating relationships. When you're dating, and even living together, there's always an easy path out of the relationship. You live with that possibility every day, so it's easier to accept when one partner opts out. Even in this age of easy divorce, a marriage commitment promises to be forever.

Intertwining of lives. To what extent have the two of you been involved in each other's daily lives? If you only saw your spouse on weekends, as you both jetted around on business trips, then the breakup will probably be less painful. Those whose lives have been constantly connecting and intertwining will suffer a greater loss.

Shock of loss. One man learns that his wife has cancer, and he mourns with her for the last three years of her life. Another loses his wife suddenly in a car accident. The accidental death will require more time afterward for healing. The first man actually does much of the healing together with his wife before she passes. Denial, anger, bargaining, and some depression can all occur beforehand. He might continue in depression for a short time after her death, but acceptance should come fairly soon. Yet a sudden death will throw the surviving spouse into denial and anger for a good long time.

Possibility of renewed relationship. This is why divorce generally takes longer for healing than bereavement. With bereavement, the mourning partner can't spend much time in the bargaining stage because he or she knows the spouse is not coming back. The pain is sharper but irrevocable. Yet many divorces have a prolonged period of bargaining. Even if the departing spouse gives no hint of wanting reconciliation, the other spouse might devise all sorts of plans to get back together. As long as the possibility of a renewed relationship exists, it will be tough to accept a breakup.

Reopening of wounds. Ex-partners know how to push your buttons. And they will. If there's an extended divorce proceeding, if you share custody or visitation of children, or if you continue to move in the same social circles, your buttons will get pushed. It can be difficult to move past the anger and bargaining stages. In such cases, depression is actually a blessing. It tends to isolate a person, removing him or her from the contacts that would stir up old feelings.

Quality of recovery. This is a catch-all category, but the point remains: Some people heal well and others don't. Each stage of the recovery process has a purpose, and recovery proceeds best when those stages are allowed to run their courses. Some people fight each new stage; others go with the flow. Your progress will be faster if you allow each new stage to happen. Ignore those well-meaning friends who want to keep you from feeling angry or depressed, or try to push you along faster than you need to go. Let the process happen.

Support network. We've criticized "well-meaning friends" in these pages, but supportive friends are crucial in your recovery time. You need people who'll be sensitive to your emotional needs, who understand the process you need to go through. You need listeners rather than preachers. We like the story of Job in the Bible. He suffered great losses to his family and fortune. As he sat mourning on the trash pile, three friends came and sat with him. For a week. Now that's friendship: to sit on the trash pile with a suffering buddy. Then they started talking, trying to figure out why Job was suffering and telling him what to do about it. They should have just kept quiet (which is what God tells them later). It's enough for a friend to simply sit with you; you don't need friends who try to fix things.

When you go to the doctor with a broken arm, he or she will put it in a cast and say, "Come back and see me in three weeks."

What do you do during those three weeks to make your healing go faster? Nothing. Your arm's in a cast, immobilized. You could probably crack open the cast every few days to see how the healing is going. But it wouldn't help. You really have to wait and let the healing happen.

The same is true of your emotional healing. The more you try to rush the process, the more you delay it. Let the healing happen.

While waiting is difficult, it has some valuable side effects. Camp out at a supermarket some time and watch people in the checkout lines. Some obviously hate to wait. They shift their feet and drum their fingers and sigh loudly as the teenage clerk calls for a price check on Pampers. But others seem serene about it. Perhaps they've already allotted time for this situation. They expect to wait in line. Perhaps they're using that time to do breathing exercises, to meditate, or to catch up on the tabloid headlines. All the finger drumming in the world won't make the line go any faster. It'll only raise your blood pressure.

The same is true of your emotional healing. You might as well enjoy the wait. Expect it. Accept it. And embrace it. Use it. You have enough pain from the breakup itself. Don't compound it by fuming or worrying about how long your recovery is taking. Receive the gifts that this recovery time is giving you.

Time gives you rest. We all need "down time." That's why we take vacations—well, some of us anyway. In fact, when you push yourself too hard, too long, your body will break down in some way. You need a break.

After you experience an emotional wound, you need rest. Your mind and spirit are racing through denial and anger and bargaining. That all takes a lot of energy. And it's why you eventually take the "forced vacation" of depression. You need to shut down for a while. Instead of scolding yourself for not doing more, accept this down time as a needed break. If you need to come home from work and veg out in front of the TV every night, do it! Your emotions need the rest.

If you've ever had an appendix or gall bladder removed, you know there's a recovery process. Apparently, these organs aren't that important, but they've been removed from your body. Even when you've been sewn back together, you need time to rest so your body can regain its strength. Emotionally, after a divorce you've had a piece of your heart removed. You might decide that you're better off without it, but still you've been wounded, and you need to rest—physically and emotionally. Take the time to do so.

Time enlarges your focus. In the immediate aftermath of a breakup, there are two people you care about—yourself and your ex. The rest of the planet might as well be . . . well . . . a different planet. As your ex fades into history, there's just one person in your consciousness—you. There's nothing wrong with this. Because of your wounds, your mind naturally constricts to focus on your own needs, your own feelings, and your own recovery. But this might make you oversensitive about how others are treating you, and undersensitive about how you're treating them. You might fly off the handle over some minor mistreatment that you receive (or even only perceive). But you might be oblivious to the way you're treating others.

Over time, your focus will grow to include those around you. You'll gain a more balanced perspective about your own needs and those of others.

Time helps you get all the facts. When Keith's wife said she needed more, he believed her. He began to see himself as inadequate.

But over time, he began to see the pattern that had always existed in their relationship. She'd always wanted more. He was always sacrificing for her, but she never did much for him. The truth wasn't that he was unable to satisfy a wife, it was that his wife was unable to be satisfied.

In a similar way, our friend Dawn beat herself up after her husband left her for another woman. She felt she had failed him as a wife, forcing him to look elsewhere. But over time she learned that he had carried on several affairs during their marriage. She wasn't a failure; he was a cheat!

On the other hand, time might help you gain a truer understanding of yourself. Especially in the anger stage, blame gets thrown about freely. After his divorce, Tom's counselor asked him, "What did you do to make her leave?" Tom was aghast. Wasn't the counselor listening? Didn't he realize that Tom's wife was the culprit here and Tom the victim? It was only years later that Tom began to ask himself the same question.

Over time, you can get past the blame and start seeing the real issues. It's not about who wears the white hat and who wears the black hat. As you heal, you can look more honestly at your own role in the breakup. If you change the way you act in a relationship, that might help you in future connections.

Time lets you see how things turn out. Sharon tearfully told her circle of friends that Alex had broken up with her after three years of dating and even living together for a while. The friends consoled her, but after she left, they turned to one another and said, "It's about time!" Truth was, Alex was awful for her—demanding and detracting. For some reason, Sharon was hopelessly in love with him. They had all encouraged her to leave him, but she never would. Now he'd done the deed, and she was heartbroken. But her friends all knew that this was the best thing that had happened to her in a long time. Over time, she'd see that as well.

Many people have stories of lost jobs, lost opportunities, or lost relationships that turned out for the best. Randy's loss of an editing job launched his freelance career. Tom's painful divorce put him in a position where later he could lead a divorce-recovery group and write books like this one.

You never really know how things would have been if those jobs or relationships continued. In the wake of a traumatic loss, we all tend to think the future looks bleak. But over time, the future unfolds more brightly than we expect.

Time allows you to balance out your life. George came home from a business trip to an empty house. The problem was, he was married at the time. But his wife had grown tired of his frequent travels and had taken a lover who paid more attention to her. Now she'd moved in with him. At first George ranted and raved over her infidelity, but eventually he realized that he'd made his job into his lover. He recalled various hints his wife dropped along the way—hints he ignored. It was too late now to save that marriage, but George realized that his life was lopsided—all work and no play.

As in George's case, the loss of a relationship can often be a wake-up call. After the flush of anger, people sometimes realize their own imbalances. Maybe they've been too selfish, too serious, too frivolous, too lazy, too talkative, and too quiet.

During their time of recovery, many people rediscover their spiritual side. They start to pray more. They wonder why God would let this happen. Maybe they haven't thought about God since second-grade Sunday school, but now they sense how meaningful it is to have a relationship with him. They'd cruised along in their train of personal success. But now that the train is derailed, they have time to re-evaluate things. What are they doing? Why are they doing it?

This spiritual awakening serves to round out their lives. And it would never happen unless they'd been forced to take the time to re-evaluate.

REBOUNDS

Christine had been married fifteen years and expected to be married fifty more. But one day, her husband Mike announced that he was divorcing her. She assumed he'd found another woman, though he never admitted it. He was very businesslike about the whole matter. As he had always done in their marriage, he took control of their divorce. And she let him. Christine would have to assume the rent and car payments, but she could also keep the furniture. He tried to lessen his own guilt by allowing her life to go on pretty much as it had before — except now she was poorer and single.

Their lives had always revolved around the church — they'd taught Sunday school together. He gallantly volunteered to leave the church so she could retain that network of friends, but that was the church he'd grown up in. His parents still worshiped there. No, she had no desire to undergo the scrutiny of those prying eyes ("Wonder what she did to make him go?"). She said that she'd find another church.

So she went alone to a new church, sitting quietly in the back pew, making few new friends. Except one guy showed an interest in her. Rick was active in the church, very thoughtful, encouraging. Just like her ex-husband, only nicer.

When Rick began asking her out, she said no at first. She didn't think she was ready. But he kept asking, and Christine finally agreed. Her husband had left her feeling ugly, unwanted, unworthy of anyone's attention. And now this great guy was complimenting her, wanting to be with her. She couldn't believe it.

Christine was determined to go slow with this relationship, but Rick was exactly what she needed. She began to get emotionally attached. Though she had drawn strict sexual boundaries in their relationship, she was soon giving in to his advances, going further than she wanted. It was all moving forward very fast.

How do you think this story ends? You probably know someone like Christine. Maybe you are someone like Christine. Anyway, you can finish this story in several ways — few of them with happy endings.

In some stories, Rick would be a user — maybe intentionally, maybe not. Some guys prey on wounded women, taking advantage of their emotional weakness. (And some women prey on wounded men.) Other guys don't mean to be mean, but they find themselves drawn to needy women. As a result, the relationships are always one-sided — one partner meeting the other's needs. That can't be healthy.

Often, in a rebound relationship like this, the story would end with Christine getting too attached to Rick — and eventually Rick would break up with her. Then all the pain of both breakups would afflict her, and Christine would be even worse off.

As it happened, Rick was an unintentional user, wanting to meet Christine's needs, but soon finding that he wasn't getting enough from this one-sided relationship. He didn't want to hurt her more by breaking up with her, but he became emotionally distant. This was greatly frustrating for Christine. It was a different kind of pain, a prolonged feeling of the same old inadequacy, but it still hurt. After about a year of dating, Christine realized that this rebound relationship wasn't helping her any, so she broke up with Rick.

Rebound relationships are hazardous to your health. They're extremely tempting, but rarely does anything good come out of them. We can't say this strongly enough: Do not get into rebound relationships. You'll think you're the exception — that you've found the perfect person to make you forget about old so-and-so. You'll expect that "all you need is love," and that this new person will wipe away your tears. Forget about it. It's not going to happen like that.

The hard truth is that you can't handle a new relationship for a couple of years after a major breakup.

You're too fragile. You ought to be wearing a "handle with care" label on your back. The slightest slight will send you tumbling. If you get into a new relationship and your new partner so much as looks at you cross-eyed, you'll fall apart. It's just not worth the risk. We know people who have skipped from one romance to another for a decade or more, but they've never really recovered from the first breakup. Give yourself time to get better.

You're too needy. You think this wonderful new person you met will meet all your needs, but you have more needs than either of you know about. You're an extremely high-maintenance personality right now. Even if this wonder-mate of yours does manage to meet most of your needs — what kind of relationship is that? One-sided. It's all about you. When you do recover, you'll be ready for a more balanced relationship, but your partner probably won't be. So you'll either stay in an unhealthy imbalance or you'll break up, which will simply send you back into recovery.

Your expectations are too high. You're trusting in your new partner to save you from all the grief you've gone through. No matter how great that man or woman is, it won't happen like that. You have to work through the old issues. You have to walk that narrow trail from denial to acceptance. No one else can do that for you.

There are too many users out there. As you recover, you're vulnerable. And some people can sniff out vulnerability an area code away. Some are just nasty. They'll use you for sex or money or sport and leave you worse off than you were before. Others might truly want to help you, but they're addicted to one-sided relationships. Both of these types are dangerous, and you usually can't recognize them before it's too late.

You can't see straight. Your perceptions are clouded by the pain you've been through. You feel so needy that you're likely to grab anyone with a pulse. In your recovery condition, you're not a good judge of character. Especially after the demise of your previous relationship, you need to be sure the next one is well thought out. Work on your own recovery for a couple of years before you start looking for a new partner.

We're not saying you need to coop yourself up and never have fun. Sure, get out there with your friends and have a good time. Find that handful of friends—or just one—who can encourage you, challenge you, and keep you on the right path. But be very careful about your relationships with people of the opposite sex. If you get into a relationship with someone of the opposite gender, keep things platonic. Avoid situations where you'll be tempted to get romantically or sexually involved.

In a way, we're suggesting that you treat yourself as you'd treat a twelve-year-old daughter or niece. "Go out and have fun with the group, but you're not ready for a serious romance yet. Maybe in a couple of years."

Maybe you know someone who had surgery and tried to come back too soon. The result: relapse. We often read of sports stars who push their recovery too hard and wind up re-injuring themselves. You need to take time for proper healing. Of course, you want to be all better. You'd love to wake up tomorrow and have it all behind you. But healing takes time. If you never take the time, you'll need to heal all over again. And again. And again. Allow yourself time now for proper recovery, and get it over with.

TIMELINE REMINDER

We discussed this earlier, but most people wonder when they should be moving from stage to stage during the recovery process. Of course, since every person is different, it's hard to say precisely. It also depends on when you start the clock.

Sometimes a breakup happens suddenly. Your significant other drops a bombshell: He or she has decided not to be significant to you any more. The shock hits you then, and you might be in for a lengthy period of denial.

But what if you've been having problems for several months or a year? You've already been dabbling in several of the stages. The ultimate breakup isn't a shock; it might even be a relief. There's still some recovery time afterward, but it's not prolonged.

We often see two partners at different levels of the process. Say Jim is considering asking Mary for a divorce. He goes through inner turmoil for a year or two, passing through all those stages, and finally he tells her. That marks the end of the process for him, but it may just be the beginning for her. In the following months, she might wonder how he can be so carefree when she's such a mess. "I guess he never really cared for me," she moans. Not so. He just went through his "mess" privately a year earlier.

From the point of impact—your first serious awareness that you'll be breaking up—count on at least two years of recovery. Often it takes more; very rarely less. Here's how the recovery times stack up for various crises:

- Death of a spouse or close family member—two to three years
- Loss of a valued job—one to two years
- Divorce—two to five years
- Broken trust: affair/betrayal—one to five years
- Broken engagement—one to two years
- Breakup of dating relationship—three months to one year

REAL LIFE STORIES
JANINE TURNER & MARIE

Janine Turner

She's not a household name, but she created an unforgettable character on the popular TV series *Northern Exposure*. Janine Turner played Maggie O'Connell, the tough, independent-minded pilot. The actress now says that role was similar to the role she's currently playing in real life. She's a single mother with no contact at all with the father of three-year-old Juliette. In fact, the child's father has never even seen her. Turner was seven months pregnant when he left, never to return.

Her relationship with this man had seemed so loving. She fully expected to start this family together. As you might expect, when he walked out she was frightened, angry, and deeply saddened. Of course, the Hollywood thing to do would be to jump into another romantic relationship and get the tabloids buzzing. Or deny the pain by throwing yourself into another TV show or movie. You might recall that she was a rising star at the time. Smart and pretty, she could have had her pick of creative projects. But Turner was smart enough to know she was deeply wounded. She took time out to heal herself and to raise her daughter.

About three years. That's the time Janine Turner stepped out of the limelight, for the good of herself and her child. In the entertainment biz, that's an eternity. How many starlets have zoomed past her? How many movie execs are saying, "Janine who?" But that's the time it took for her to heal. Only recently has she begun taking movie roles again.

Religious faith played an important part in Turner's decision to raise her daughter solo and to put her career on a back burner. She considers her child a true blessing who has helped her heal from the disappointment of her failed relationship. Her time alone with Juliette, free from the encumbrance of other relationships, has helped her become stronger, even though she's shed tears in the process. She still has moments of near-panic, when she complains that she has to do it all herself. But she knows that she has taken the wise path of healing. She needed time, and she took it.

> *"There are many events in the womb of time which will be delivered."*
>
> —Shakespeare, *Othello*

Marie

Marie heard Tom talk about the need to allow time for recovery and she took him seriously. Maybe too seriously. After hearing that it's wise to wait two years after a divorce before dating again, she circled the two-year point on her calendar. Even though there was a nice man showing interest in her about a year after her divorce, she refused to reciprocate. But then the two-year date arrived and she immediately changed her tune with this guy, letting him know that she'd like to date him.

The relationship progressed in a sensible fashion—not too fast. Marie was determined that this wouldn't be a classic "rebound" romance. But every so often she'd be troubled by something in this new relationship. The guy got talking about his car, and she flashed back to her former husband, who was insanely devoted to his car. She suddenly felt anxious about this new relationship, even though she knew that made no sense. Her teenage kids were another factor. They had been urging her to date again during her two-year hiatus, but now that she was involved with this guy, they weren't so sure. Marie was very bothered by their cool feelings toward her new beau. She had expected everything to be perfect. After all, she had waited two years! She came to Tom for help.

Tom assured her that she was normal. The two-year period is not some magic elixir. People will still have problems after that. Starting a new relationship after an old one didn't work out is always taxing, no matter how long you wait. But Tom commended Marie for her discipline. Imagine how serious her problems would be if she hadn't waited that long!

4

SLIPPERY SLOPE

ReStart Principle 4:
Healing is a slippery slope.

EARLY in life we learn to chart our progress toward a goal. A first-grade student is just starting out on the road to graduation. A sixth-grade student is halfway there. By the twelfth grade, a student is almost ready for that diploma. We always know where we stand.

But imagine what would happen if we placed the grades in random order. What if a six-year-old started in the fourth grade, then moved into second, seventh, or tenth, depending on the whim of the teacher? It would be chaos. And yet that's kind of what happens along the way from denial to acceptance when you're starting over. You might expect a clear, step-by-step progression—spend two months in denial, then "graduate" to anger for another three months, then step up to bargaining. People like us often make it seem very orderly.

The truth is, you're climbing a slippery slope. Move up two stages, fall back one. You might go through all the stages on the same day, then start all over the next morning. You're still making progress, but it's hard to tell that at any given moment.

As Easy as Climbing a Rock!

Rock climbing has enjoyed a certain popularity in recent years, and it gives us a great picture of the recovery process. The rock climber's goal is to ascend a steep crag, and he or she does so by searching for crevices, indentations, and ledges—anything to grab onto. Sometimes a climber will go quite a way up a rock face and then determine that there are no more handholds or footholds above that point—no way to keep climbing directly upward. So the climber climbs down or across, often giving up hard-earned height. Why? To find a better way up. Eventually the climber scales the rock, but not in a straight line. If you were to map the climber's path up the rock face, you would see many twists and turns and backtracks.

That's how the map of recovery looks.

Then what's all this talk about stages? Is there, or is there not, a progression from denial to anger to bargaining to depression to acceptance to forgiveness?

There is, but it's not a steady climb. You can expect to move backward from time to time, yet you should experience a general progression forward.

It's all very fluid, but there is still progress. What you need to keep reminding yourself is this: You will slip back. Everyone does. Don't get discouraged when it happens to you, when it keeps happening to you. That only means you're normal.

There's a game called Jenga with wooden blocks of various shapes and sizes. The goal is to build a tower of these blocks, perching one precariously on top of another. Of course, eventually, someone tries to balance some piece that won't stay put, and the whole structure comes crashing down. Make one mistake and you have to start all over. Fortunately, recovery isn't like that. One little setback doesn't ruin the whole thing. You can usually get back on track fairly quickly.

TOM'S SLIPPERY SLOPE

Tom had a significant "slippery slope" period four years after his divorce. (It's not uncommon to slip back even after you've reached acceptance.) It had to do with Tom's future education. After wallowing a while in the depression stage, Tom decided he should put his life back together. That would involve going back to school and getting a graduate degree. So he began to plan, choosing the best school for him.

Now he had to call the school for an application. This turned out to be incredibly difficult. Each day he told himself he'd have to call, but first it was too early, then he'd have other things to do. Then it was lunchtime, and then he'd forget until late afternoon, probably too late to call. This went on for weeks. It was a simple task to pick up the phone and call, but he was filled with anxiety.

Surely he'd recovered from his divorce by now! But he was slipping back into the depression, into some bargaining (would that degree impress his ex?), and he even felt some of that old anger against the wife who left him. This emotional hodge-podge kept him from calling the school for quite a while, but he finally did.

Then he had to fill out the application. That would be easy enough, right? Wrong. It lay on the dining-room table for months. Many times, Tom walked right past it and scolded himself. "Gotta get to that . . . tomorrow." But it didn't get done in a pack of tomorrows.

Considering what Tom had been through, the application was

more daunting than you'd expect. Basically, he had to explain his life on this piece of paper, telling them why he was worthy of their commitment to him. It was a proposal of sorts, and that hadn't worked so well before. What if they rejected him? Then he'd be certain that he was utterly useless.

After months of procrastination, he actually filled out the application and sent it in. Then he was afraid to check the mail. He'd be relieved each time he did not get a reply from the school. No rejection yet. But one day the school's response arrived. Tom tore open the letter and read: "We regret to inform you . . ."

He felt as if he'd been punched in the gut. Rejected again! He'd told them everything they needed to know about him, and they didn't want him. How dare they! His anger raged against the school, and then against his ex-wife: "If it weren't for her, I wouldn't be in this mess!" The same anger, bargaining, and depression he'd already worked through in the past four years was consuming him again.

But the story doesn't end there. Tom had been through those stages and he knew the way out. When he started railing against his ex-wife, he stopped himself. "This isn't about her. This is my business." His forays into bargaining and depression were brief because he didn't need to go there this time. He was having a setback, but a temporary one.

Within a week, he was trying again, researching other schools and meeting with an adviser to help him in the application process.

We've learned from Alcoholics Anonymous that recovery is an ongoing process. That's why people say, "I'm a recovering alcoholic," not "a former alcoholic." The danger of relapse is always there, but you take one day at a time and keep moving forward.

A breakup is quite different from alcoholism, of course, but the recovery processes have similarities. For quite a while after a breakup, even after you think you're "cured," you're still in danger of slipping back down the slope. But if you do, at least you know the way back. You can grab those handholds and pull yourself back up.

Why do we slip back? What causes our relapses? Several factors, some of which are unavoidable. But others we can learn to recognize and manage, to make sure our slips don't set us back too far.

SPARKS

This is our term for those events and people that spark our anger, frustration, denial, or depression. Holidays are classic sparks, as you can't help but recall the better times that you spent together (or perhaps the fights you used to have during holidays). You might spend an evening with old friends, people you used to visit along with your spouse. Now you're alone and, while everyone tries to avoid the subject, you can't help but think of your breakup.

Obviously, if you interact with your ex on a regular basis, perhaps regarding childcare, each meeting has the potential to bring back memories or issues. But the children themselves can spark some old feelings, as you see the effects of the breakup on them.

Places you used to travel together, your ex's old office building, the shop where you used to pick up bagels for Sunday brunch—these can all set you back. The shoes you bought for your anniversary party, a comb you find between the cushions of the couch, even smells that remind you of the good old days— practically anything can be a spark that ignites some old passion.

Such sparks take you back in time and force you to move

through the stages of recovery all over again. Maybe a wistful thought makes you feel as if the breakup never happened. That's denial, and you'll have to re-convince yourself that it did. That might make you angry again, and so on.

Maybe some comment your ex makes while dropping off the kids stirs up your anger. You think, That's exactly why we broke up! I can't stand that! And suddenly you're dredging up all the hurtful things he or she ever did to you, fighting battles decided long ago. You're back in the anger stage, and you may need to proceed through some bargaining and depression to get out.

Or maybe you see your ex and actually have a civil discussion. "Just like old times. Why did we ever break up?" Suddenly you're thinking, "If only . . ." and "Why didn't we ever . . . ?" and "Maybe we could still . . ." That's bargaining, as you imagine this one polite conversation could begin to undo all the damage that has been done.

(By the way, don't get us wrong. We love it when separated couples reunite, building a healthy new relationship after working through the issues that drove them apart. But when there has been a serious breach, holding out hope of a reconciliation is usually just an unhealthy pipe dream that delays true recovery.)

Perhaps you go out for dinner with your parents, but you go home in a funk. You'll never make them happy. Where did they go wrong? You'll never succeed in a relationship. There's no hope for you. Some parents can be strongly supportive, but others can spark feelings of inadequacy. This can send you back into a depression that you'll have to climb out of.

What can you do to keep these sparks from igniting problems in your recovery?

Avoid them when you're weak. If you're feeling emotionally vulnerable, drive a mile out of your way to avoid passing a memory-laden park. It's okay to send regrets to a wedding invitation if that event would tear you apart. You don't need to hang out with all the couples you and your ex used to party with. Eventually, you'll be able to handle all of that, but as you're recovering you might need to say no. Learn to monitor your own emotional strength, and when you're weak, be careful.

Ask them for help. If your sparks are people, try to be direct with them. Ask your children not to talk so much about your ex. Ask your parents to be more supportive. Ask your friends to understand that you feel awkward at couples' events. You might even ask your ex to stay away for a while. Remember: You're needy right now. People will give you some space.

Talk yourself out of trouble. Especially if you're walking into a den of lions, be ready to lecture yourself back to sanity. Write the story of your recovery and memorize it. Seriously! Write something like: I tried hard to make things work with my ex, but he or she walked out anyway. I'm far from perfect, but this wasn't my fault. Yes, I deserved better treatment, but I'm not going to dwell on that. The past is past, and the future is full of possibilities. With God's help, I'm going to build a great new life for myself. A simple statement like that, including things you've learned during your recovery, will help you get back on track after a slip up.

Build new associations. Create new memories to replace the old ones. Make new friends on your own and spend at least as much time with them as you spend with your "couple" friends. Redeem some of those old special places or events by doing fun things with your new friends.

Get outside support. Find at least one special friend who will be on call for you. When you encounter a spark, call that friend.

With serious setbacks, you might see a professional counselor, but in most cases a friend can talk you back to earth.

Recovery Incomplete

Another reason you might slip back in your recovery is that you didn't get a certain stage right the first time. Sometimes people try to speed up the recovery process, moving toward acceptance when they're really not ready yet. Sometimes it's the people around you who do the hurrying. "You should be over that by now, shouldn't you?"

At one divorce-recovery seminar, Tom met a woman who exuded good cheer. She listened sympathetically to others, spoke wisely during the discussion, and seemed to encourage everyone she met. Tom was stunned to learn that her husband had left her just two months earlier. Yet here she was, giving every indication that she was solidly in the acceptance stage. He asked her about the stages of recovery, which he had just spoken about in the seminar, and she shrugged and said she must have gone through them very quickly.

Flash-forward one year. Same site. Another seminar. And here was this same woman, now looking very discouraged. Gone was the cheerful spirit. The bouncy certainty that had encouraged others the year before was nowhere to be seen. "Now I am in the pit," she said. "I don't have anything to offer anyone."

Tom was saddened, but not surprised. It's practically impossible to go through the stages of recovery in two months. If you rush through a stage, you'll have to go back and make it up later. That's what happened to this woman.

We don't mean to criticize people for "not getting it right the first time." That's not a failing on your part. The process is different for everyone, and we each bring our own personality to it. Some stages are more difficult for some people.

For example, some people have no problem with anger. They've learned to express their rage fully and freely. They'll yell at someone one minute and hug him the next. Others feel inhibited in expressing anger. They've learned that "nice" people control their negative emotions. So they bottle up their feelings, not even allowing themselves to feel angry. Such people might have to revisit the anger stage several times along their route of recovery, each time expressing more and more of their true feelings.

Other people have difficulty with depression. Well, everyone has difficulty with depression in a way, but these people are afraid of it or opposed to it. We suspect the woman Tom met at the seminar was like this. She was very good at being cheerful, but embarrassed about being depressed. Some people learn a "put on a happy face" attitude that keeps them from being honest when they're down. Others avoid depression because they fear where it might lead them. Isolation. Drug abuse. Suicide. They don't know where that dark tunnel leads, so they won't set foot in it. They pretend to rush past depression into acceptance, but it won't work like that. They'll keep coming back to depression even after they think they've recovered.

What can you do about slip-backs like this? Maybe nothing. Those reversions are just making sure you serve your full sentence. Accept them without panic, and allow yourself to go through the stages fully, even if this is a return engagement. Otherwise, your life might become something like the movie *Groundhog Day*, with each stage being re-lived until you get it right.

But here are some ideas for making the best of it.

Educate your family and friends. Let them know about the stages of recovery and what they can expect from you. Give them a reasonable timetable. If they know you're expected to go through these stages for a couple of years, they probably won't rush you through it as much.

Create controlled environments for difficult emotions. Punching a pillow is the classic "controlled environment" for anger. You release your feelings without hurting anyone. Or get a friend to do role-play with you (but no punching). If you're afraid of depression, get friends to check up on you. Allow yourself to be miserable in their company. (They'll understand!)

Enjoy the process as much as possible. Enjoy the process? Sounds a bit silly, but it is possible. Keep a diary of your recovery, and reread it from time to time. This can help you see your progress. On some nights, review the day and see how many of the stages you hit. It's really true that many people go through all the stages in the same day, especially in the middle of the process.

NEW INFORMATION

Sometimes you learn something new about the facts of your breakup. That will almost certainly cause a relapse, since you have a whole new event to make peace with.

Bill's wife left him, saying she didn't "feel fulfilled" in the marriage. He begged Lisa to tell him how he could make her feel fulfilled, but she was already out the door. In the aftermath, he agonized over what he'd done wrong. A year later, his wife's best friend let it slip that Lisa had been having an affair with a man at work before she left Bill. This put everything in a new light. It wasn't just his own failings as a husband anymore—Lisa had been unfaithful and wanted to pursue a new relationship.

New information like that might seem to make recovery easier, but it can also throw you back into some previous stages. Bill became very angry, as you might expect, because the first time through there wasn't as much to be angry about.

Donna's fiancé, Justin, left her for his "ideal woman." He brutally explained to Donna all the magnificent details of his new dream girl. Maybe he wanted her to understand and give her blessing. In any case, Donna spent several months berating herself for being not as pretty, not as young, not as educated—until she learned that he had dumped the ideal woman after six weeks to pursue a more ideal woman. Obviously, Justin had a problem, and Donna was just so much flotsam left in his wake.

This new information made Donna's recovery a bit easier, but it temporarily threw her back into anger and a curious bout of bargaining ("He needs someone like me to teach him true love").

You might learn that something you did or said unwittingly sent your spouse packing. You might learn that a third party told lies about you or your spouse. You might discover that your ex was a con artist, an alcoholic, or an abuser. This news might make his or her actions more understandable or more heinous. It might make you feel better about yourself or worse. It might create a possibility for reunion or slam the door shut forever. But whatever new information you get, it redefines the event, forcing you to respond to it all over again.

What can you do to keep new information from tripping you up too badly? Ask yourself a few questions.

What does it change? Be clear on the redefinition. What exactly has changed? Your understanding of the breakup. Perhaps you have a better handle on the reasons for the breakup. Perhaps you know more about yourself or your ex. Some things have changed, but not everything. There was still a breakup. There was still pain. You still need to recover from this event. Be precise in your new understanding.

Is there seriously any possibility of reunion? The biggest problem with new information is that it might give you false hope of getting back together. If you've fought your way through denial, the last thing you need is a hint of reunion. When the new information serves to excuse or lessen the offense, the recovering partner is often thrown back into the bargaining—seeking quick fixes for an old relationship. In a very few cases, the new information might reopen a real possibility of getting back together. If that's your situation, go for it. But be careful. You must look this issue squarely in the eye. Gather your wisest friends around you and run it by them. Does this really mean the breakup is reversible? Probably not.

What can I learn about myself? New information usually helps you see yourself and your ex in a new light. It doesn't really matter how you see your ex right now, but you might learn some valuable things about yourself. What sort of person are you attracted to? How do you function in a relationship? The new data might give you new insights that will help your recovery and your future life.

PRIDE OR FEAR

These tandem emotions can short-circuit the recovery process, forcing a slip back down the slope. In both cases, you don't really want to go through the recovery process, so you sabotage it.

Proud people think they're above this recovery business. "Two years? I'll be fine in a week." Eager to show their success in dealing with the breakup, they gloss right over the anger, bargaining, and depression stages. They look like they've accepted the situation, but looks are deceiving. They'll keep slipping back to these stages until they finally submit.

Recovery can be humiliating. To lash out in anger, to grasp for easy answers, or to feel the crushing sadness of depression—these can embarrass a proud person. You don't want to admit to anyone that your ex broke your heart and threw your emotions out of whack, but that's the truth. Own up to it.

Fear can also cause slip-backs. Some people are afraid to step into a future without their former partner. They can't imagine what that would be like. It seems scary to go through life alone. And so they keep going backward. As long as they're burning with anger or sunk in depression, they don't have to deal with the future. The stages of recovery at least keep them emotionally connected to their past, so they'd rather stay there.

What can you do to keep pride and fear from pulling you backward?

Find one person to be honest with. If you can't find someone among your family and friends, then see a counselor. But you need to have someone you can drop the façade with. If pride is keeping you from recovering fully, then find someone who knows all your foibles and keep that person informed as you go from stage to stage. Allow yourself to be a struggler in this person's eyes. You don't need this confidant to coach or advise you, just to listen—and maybe to see through your self-serving excuses.

If fear is holding you back, you still need a confidant, but one who will quietly encourage you onward. Misery loves company, but what you don't need right now is someone who will merely confirm how terrible things are. You need a bit of a cheerleader. Try to find such a person (or see such a counselor) and be honest about your struggle.

Take pride in your honesty. Especially if pride is holding you back, try a different angle. The problem is that you don't want to look like a loser, so you never fully enter the stages of recovery. But what if you decided to win through honesty? By being honest with yourself about the pain you feel, you can work through the recovery process, struggling at each stage and yet emerging victorious. If you don't want to look like a loser, fine! Then take pride in winning—but you need to win over something. That is, you have to enter the struggle. If you don't admit to any problems, then that's a shallow victory. It's like the New York Mets winning the Little League World Series. Big deal! A pro team defeats a bunch of kids! But if you stand up against fierce competition and come out a winner, that's something you can truly take pride in.

Find role models in those who have gone through it. Seek out people you know who were divorced five or ten years ago. Talk to them about their struggles. If pride is your problem, this will help you see a new kind of winner to emulate. If fear is holding you back, then this will give you a vision of a post-breakup life that might inspire you. Yes, there will be a future for you, so you don't need to dawdle in recovery.

We want to re-emphasize this: You're on a slippery slope. You will slip back from time to time. Don't panic. You can still make your way, one handhold at a time, up the steep rockface of recovery. Stop looking around and comparing yourself with others. Each person's path is different. You'll zig-zag through the stages, but pretty soon you'll realize that denial isn't an issue anymore. And then you'll notice that you haven't slipped back to anger for a while. Gradually, you'll find yourself further up the face of the rock, and soon you'll be on top of the world.

REAL LIFE STORIES

└──► JULIA ROBERTS & BECKY

Julia Roberts

Most women, whether they admit it or not, would give any-thing to be in Julia Roberts' shoes. Rich, famous, thin, and beautiful, she has what many people think they need in order to be happy in this life. How could anyone be as perfect as Julia Roberts and not be on top of the world?

But apparently, wealth and beauty don't guarantee hap-piness and a life free from struggles. Roberts has had the same kinds of relationship woes that anyone else has; the names are just better known.

In 1993, just three weeks after they met, Julia married singer Lyle Lovett in an outdoor ceremony where the bride went barefoot. Both the bride and groom were on the rebound — Julia had just broken up with Kiefer Sutherland, whom she had been scheduled to marry, and Lovett was recovering from a failed romance with Allison Inman. Before that, Julia had been engaged to Dylan McDermott, after liv-ing with Liam Neeson. This background of broken relationships did not bode well for the marriage, and after twenty-one months, much of which was spent apart, Julia and Lyle announced plans to separate. Eventually they divorced.

According to close friends, Julia was deeply hurt by the breakup of the marriage. In spite of the short time she'd known Lyle, she had high hopes that their marriage would last. They'd even spoken of having children. She went through periods where she would lash out angrily at anyone who asked her about the failure of the relationship, then break into tears at the drop of a hat. She slipped into a deep depression, even refusing to attend the Oscar ceremonies. Then suddenly she was dating Daniel Day-Lewis, a handsome actor. Then it was Matthew Perry, then Pat Mannochia, a former hockey player. She couldn't seem to make up her mind whether she was angry, happy, depressed, or what.

We want to avoid diagnosing celebrities from afar. Tabloids already do too much of that. But Roberts presents a clear picture of the slippery slope of recovery. We're guessing that this string of highly publicized romances, along with the pressure of stardom, put Roberts on an emotional roller coaster, slipping through the stages but never recovering fully. Many people do this kind of thing—seeking a new relationship that will heal the pain of the old one. But there's no substitute for your own emotional processes. No one else, even the most perfect lover, can do the healing for you. New relationships, like the ones Roberts had, tend to be short-lived because of the enormous pressure placed on them. And when those new relationships end, the person goes slip-sliding away back down that slope.

At this writing, Julia Roberts seems to have settled down in a new, longer-lasting relationship with actor Benjamin Bratt. As far as we can tell, their relationship is based on close friendship, as well as romantic love, and a sharing of common interests. Perhaps she is moving forward again on the road to acceptance. We can only hope.

"It's harder to write songs when you're happy than it is when you're miserable. Who wants to hear how happy you are?"

—Lyle Lovett

Becky

Everyone in Becky's circle of friends wanted the best for her. She was such a wonderful person—outgoing, talented, friendly. Yet her friends couldn't be sure if her relationship with Ed was good for her because Becky herself didn't seem to know. They'd dated steadily for several years and at times had seemed on the road to marriage. At other times they seemed to disagree on some very basic things. Finally, Becky announced that they had broken up for good.

At first Becky was very angry with Ed, and it seemed that she wanted all of her friends to be angry with him too. She was at a normal stage on the slippery slope of recovery. She could only remember the negative aspects of their relationship and wasn't sure why she had ever been in that relationship at all.

Then she spent a Saturday evening alone.

The reality of her situation gripped her: She was no longer in a relationship. Nobody loved her. (That, of course, wasn't true, since she had a great group of loyal friends, but at that moment she wanted a man.) In the following days, Becky slid into a depression and began to cry frequently. She even began to hope that she and Ed might somehow get back together. Her friends couldn't believe their ears. Hadn't she hated this man just last week? But Becky was just at a different spot on the slippery slope.

Becky continued to slip and slide through a variety of emotions regarding her ex-boyfriend. She even dated other men in an effort to hurry up the process, but soon discovered it didn't work. She found that it filled her needs better to be with her friends or family during her recovery, rather than on a date. She also learned the value of being alone sometimes, that it doesn't need to be a frightening experience.

Becky will continue to have occasional backslides down the slippery slope, even several years after her breakup with Ed, but it has been a valuable, if difficult, learning experience for her.

5

ELUSIVE FORGIVENESS

ReStart Principle 5:
Forgiveness is essential but elusive.

"FORGIVE and forget."

"I'll never forgive her for what she did. She doesn't deserve it."

"How can you forgive that monster? That would be like saying what he did was okay!"

"Forgive him? Oh, I don't think I could ever take him back."

People have a lot of faulty ideas about forgiveness. It's an essential part of the recovery process, but its true nature is rather elusive. Many people think they've forgiven when they haven't. Others refuse to forgive because they don't understand what forgiveness really is. Let's look at some of these misconceptions.

"Forgive and forget." People hold this up as an ideal, but is it desirable or even possible? If a person wrongs you, do you really want to forget what he or she did? Even if you make peace with someone afterward, isn't the memory of the offense important information to retain?

Say a husband cheats on his wife. It was a one-night stand on a business trip, and he regrets it deeply. He comes crawling back to her, asking forgiveness. She is terribly upset, but she forgives him. Yet what should she do when he takes his next business trip? Wouldn't it be reasonable to insist that he call her every night from his hotel, just to be sure he's not tempted to stray again?

If forgetting means pretending that something never happened, that's really a dangerous bit of denial. We need to learn from all our experiences, especially the negative ones. And yet many good people claim they have forgiven and forgotten, and then they feel guilty when the memory of the offense creeps back into their minds. "I forgave that! Why does it still bother me?" They wind up playing mental hide-and-seek, trying to tuck certain memories out of reach.

CAN YOU REALLY FORGET?

"Forgive and forget" only works if we redefine forgetting. Instead of erasing something from our memory, let's think of it as choosing not to think about something. Trust us, the cheated-upon wife will not erase her husband's infidelity from her mind, but she can choose not to focus on it in their day-to-day relationship. In fact, she must make this choice, if the relationship will ever heal. Still, on certain occasions—like his next business trip—they both need to learn from the experience and take appropriate precautions.

Our deeds have consequences. Misdeeds have negative consequences. We can work to overcome them, but we can't erase them, and we shouldn't try to. You can forgive a child for throwing a bowl of pea soup across the dinner table, but for a while you'll probably also avoid wearing your finest clothes to future meals with him. And you might make him eat alone until he shows more self-control.

In the same way, the straying husband in our example has

betrayed his wife's trust. That's a very strong consequence. She might offer forgiveness, but it might still take a while for her to trust him again. By forgiving him, she declares that she won't cling to this offense as a barrier between them. She's committed to rebuilding this relationship, but she's not pretending that it doesn't need to be rebuilt. True forgiveness recognizes the continuing consequences of an offense, even while the personal grudge is released.

"I'll never forgive her for what she did. She doesn't deserve it." This statement betrays another false idea about forgiveness. No one deserves to be forgiven. If they did, it wouldn't be forgiveness, it would be . . . payment or something. The whole point of forgiveness is that you've been wronged, yet you choose not to press charges. The offender is guilty. Of course, she doesn't deserve to be forgiven. But in love and grace you offer a restored relationship.

The statement implies a kind of scorekeeping. If a person is generally good but does this one bad thing, it's assumed then that she might deserve some leeway. If that cheating husband only cheated once, but then showered his wife with gifts and good deeds, he might tip the scale in his favor. So goes the common thinking: he might deserve forgiveness in that case.

Imagine a man who gets arrested for drunk driving. On his day in court he defends himself, admitting that he drove while intoxicated, but explaining that this was one little screw-up in an amazingly good life. He talks about his Little League coaching and his contributions to civic charities; he's a good husband and father, a solid employee. Last Memorial Day he stayed up all night working on a float for the town parade. The man concludes his defense by saying, "Yes, I did it, but I throw myself on the mercy of the court. Would you really want to convict someone like me?"

The judge glares at the man and replies, "Do you want mercy or not? It sounds like you want a reward. You're saying that, because of all these great things you do, you deserve to get away with driving drunk once in a while. But you don't. You deserve punishment for irresponsibly endangering the lives of others and yourself."

The judge continues: "When a man throws himself on the mercy of the court, he's asking me to take a chance. Will this man be so moved by the mercy he receives that he'll never commit the crime again? That's what I have to determine. Sometimes it happens like that. But if I let you off easy, you might think you earned that treatment by being such a great guy. And you probably think you could earn it again. In order to receive the mercy of this court, you have to know you don't deserve it."

You can probably make that story your own, by putting names to the judge and defendant and changing the crime. Who's throwing himself or herself on your mercy? Be wary of the person who argues a case for leniency because of a good record in the past. You want the person to say, "I wronged you. I'm sorry. I don't deserve your forgiveness, but I'm asking for it anyway."

True forgiveness is a gift, not a payment. It must not excuse the crime, but just move past it. If you shrug off the offense as you try to be nice, it will come back to haunt you. Deep in your soul, you know exactly how much you've been wronged, and if you don't own up to the full severity of the crime, you will eventually return to the anger stage . . . with a vengeance. Forgiveness will drop the matter, but it has to face it first.

"How can you forgive that monster? That would be like saying what he did was okay!" Forgiveness is exactly the opposite. It's saying the behavior was not okay. If it was okay, there'd be nothing to forgive. In order to forgive, you must look squarely at the bad behavior and say, "That was bad. That was wrong. That hurt me."

Think about what would happen if you went up to a person you know casually, someone who has never done you any harm, and said, "I forgive you." What kind of reaction would you get? Puzzlement, certainly. But maybe even a touch of anger. "What do you mean you forgive me? What have I ever done to you? How dare you forgive me!" People respond like that because forgiveness implies misbehavior. Forgiveness names it, identifies it, and then chooses to let it pass.

We've seen a fascinating social experiment in recent years in South Africa. After decades of racial tension and numerous abuses, the new regime is trying a revolutionary approach: forgiveness. Led by Bishop Desmond Tutu, the Ministry of Reconciliation has sought to cool the fires of violence by offering people forgiveness—if only they will confess their crimes. Information goes along with restoration. No longer can people hide in the shadows. They must identify their abuses, but then they'll be given amnesty.

This program has had its opponents—how can you let some of these monsters go unpunished? And some wrongdoers amazingly refuse to confess and receive forgiveness. But by and large it has succeeded. Just two decades ago, international observers were predicting that South Africa would surely erupt in violence. But the transfer of power has been rather peaceful so far, largely due to this massive experiment in forgiveness.

But be very clear on this: South Africa is not shrugging off the terrible deeds that were done in racial hatred. It is clearly naming those deeds as atrocious. The nation just wants to get past it all.

You might say the same thing about interpersonal forgiveness. It's not saying it's okay to do bad things. Forgiveness calls bad things bad, but then gets past them.

"Forgive him? Oh, I don't think I could ever take him back." Many people assume that forgiveness puts a relationship right back where it was, as if the offense never happened. That's especially troubling when we're talking about divorce and romantic breakups. Forgiveness moves forward, not back. What's done is done. The question is now, "How can you live peacefully in the future?"

When a couple is still together and one partner forgives the other, the relationship can often be brought back pretty close to where it was before the offense. But even then, whatever the misdeed was, it has taught both partners new things about themselves and the relationship. They'll likely set new boundaries in the future, finding new ways to live together.

But when one partner's behavior has torn a relationship apart, forgiveness doesn't have to glue it back together. It might. It's possible that a forgiving partner could take the errant one back, but there'd still be a new kind of relationship. Maybe a better one, but definitely a different one. If you go backward, you return to a place where that behavior can and probably will happen again. If you go forward, you grow.

Let's say your partner left you two years ago for a fling with someone new. You've gone through the stages of recovery, reaching a point of acceptance. Yes, you will live to love again. And then your ex returns, spouting apologies and begging forgiveness. Should you forgive this person? Yes, that would be a good thing to work on. Should you re-establish the old relationship? No. Too much has changed. Your partner's decision two years ago set off a chain of consequences, including your pain and your subsequent growth. You're a different person now. Maybe your ex can woo you all over again, getting to know the new you and building a new relationship slowly. But you must not slip into the old relationship like a pair of well-worn slippers. That would undo a lot of the good things that have happened to you since your breakup.

We want to be careful in this discussion because we believe in marriage. In the hypothetical situation we just suggested — partner leaves, comes back, wants forgiveness — it matters a lot whether we're talking about a dating relationship or a marriage. If you were just dating the person who jilted you, tell him or her to take a hike. Seek to forgive the person in your own heart, but be wary of any future relationship. But marriage is a different case. Marriage requires a lot of forgiveness along the way, but some misdeeds — like infidelity and abandonment — can be strong enough to tear it apart. We believe an abandoned spouse has no obligation to restore the marriage, but might decide to do so (especially if it's best for the children). And yet we'd counsel such a person to avoid being manipulated by the straying spouse. Set clear boundaries in the renewed marriage. Remember: you're not going back, but going forward.

So What Is Forgiveness?

We've been talking about false ideas of forgiveness: It doesn't forget the offense; it's not deserved; it doesn't excuse the offender; it doesn't automatically restore the relationship. So what is it?

Forgiveness is a release of animosity. You have bad feelings about the person who hurt you. Some anger, some sadness, some frustration, some anxiety, and a lot of hatred. When you think of that person, this collection of bad vibes invades your soul. That's not pleasant, and it's not healthy.

By forgiving a person, you let go of those feelings. You choose not to feel that way. You allow good feelings — or at least neutral feelings — to replace the bad ones. You don't forget what happened to you, but you choose not to dwell on it. You cover over those thoughts and go about your business. You no longer plot revenge. You no longer keep a mental list of all the things your ex owes you. You no longer need to snipe at the new lover your ex is parading around with. You let go of all that.

Years ago, our friend Mary lent a car to her younger brother, Jason. He wasn't making much money at the time, but he promised to pay Mary for the car once he got established in a job. Years went by. Jason got quite well-established. Mary hinted here and there, but Jason wasn't offering to pay for the car. It became like a wall between them. At family gatherings, Mary would avoid Jason because she felt such resentment. Finally she decided that this ill feeling wasn't worth the debt of a thousand bucks or so. At the next family event she told Jason, "The car is a gift. It's yours. You don't have to pay me back." After that, she could freely enjoy Jason's company again.

What happened? Mary broke down a wall by releasing the debt. She just decided that she would stop thinking about it. In her mental record books, she wrote it off. And that action gave her back her little brother.

In the same way, forgiveness is a mental exercise. Maybe you want to perform some physical act, some ritual, to help you let it go. Write down the offense and burn the paper. Or just announce to the person that he or she is forgiven. But the main thing is to write off that debt in your mental ledger. Release it.

Forgiveness clears the way for a new relationship. As in Mary's story, forgiveness breaks down walls. It allows you to see the person, not just the offense. And it allows you to have an honest new relationship with the person you've been hating. As we've been saying, that does not mean you go back to the old relationship. Maybe it just means you can be friends. Maybe it means you can drop off the kids without crying. Maybe you'll never see your ex again, but forgiveness will mean you can think of your past relationship without slipping back down the slope.

Later we'll discuss the options for unilateral forgiveness. (Yes, you can forgive someone even if he or she has no part in your life anymore.) The emphasis here is not so much on the new relationship, but on "clearing the way." You've built a barrier, and it costs you quite a bit of energy to maintain it. At first you needed that barrier. You had to keep your tender emotions safe from any continuing damage from your ex. But now you've grown stronger. You can tear down that wall.

You see, barriers don't just protect you, they imprison you. They keep you from going where you need to go. We've talked with a number of people who struggled against forgiving their former partners, and in the meantime they found themselves unable to build meaningful new relationships with anyone else. As long as they held their grudges against those who hurt them, they were far too cautious about sharing themselves at all. You might know women who have put up barriers against all men because of the one man who hurt them. Or vice versa. Long after they've healed enough to date again, these people still refuse to give love a chance. They haven't let forgiveness tear down the wall.

So "clearing the way for a new relationship" might not even refer to a relationship with the person you're forgiving! Forgiveness, as we're describing it, is primarily a transaction within your own heart. It can free you to invest yourself in all sorts of new relationships, romantic or not.

Forgiveness is an ongoing business. Many people "forgive and forget" in entirely the wrong way. They'll forget that they've already forgiven. So, after wrestling with the issue, they'll finally release their animosity and feel the peace of forgiveness. But then a week later they remember something else their ex did, and all the bad feelings come flooding back.

It would be like Mary telling her brother the car is a gift, then calling him the next day: "So are you going to pay me or what?"

"You said it was a gift!"

"Oh. Right. Never mind."

Instead, we suggest that you forgive, and then remember that you have forgiven. Be vigilant in exorcising those feelings of hatred. As with any other stage on this slippery slope, it's easy to lose the ground we've gained by forgiving. Some people are able to flip the forgiveness switch on in their hearts and that's it. Most people struggle a bit longer with it.

Of course, forgiveness can become more difficult as you gain new information. From time to time you'll flash back to some event you had forgotten, some scene that makes your ex seem even more dastardly. Did your forgiveness cover that too? Sometimes you're like a health insurance executive searching for expenses that aren't covered. "My forgiveness covered rudeness and betrayal, but I think laziness was a pre-existing condition." When you start forgiving, you need to stay with it.

Forgiveness is an act of humility. You wouldn't expect this because forgivers usually stand on the high moral ground. "You offended me, but I'm big enough to forgive you for it." It sounds like such a proud thing. But the truth is that morally proud people have the hardest time forgiving others. They tend to be score-keepers, and they exult in their 900 to 3 lead. Forgiveness resets the score 0 to 0. That's tough for a proud person to do.

Forgiveness comes most easily to those who realize their own shortcomings. Those who know they need forgiveness themselves find it easy to drop their animosity toward people who have hurt them. Forgiven people forgive others.

Forgiveness is seeing with new eyes. In his fine book on this subject, *Forgive and Forget,* Lewis Smedes retells a European fable about a man betrayed by his wife. Fouke pretended to forgive Hilda, but he nursed bitterness in his heart. Every time he looked at her he saw only a betrayer, and he hated her for it. An angel came and told the man how to heal his hurt.

"Fouke would need the miracle of the magic eyes. He would need eyes that could look back to the beginning of his hurt and see his Hilda, not as a wife who betrayed him, but as a weak woman who needed him. Only a new way of looking at things through the magic eyes could heal the hurt flowing from the wounds of yesterday."

The man asked the angel how to get these magic eyes, and the angel responded: "Only ask, desiring as you ask, and they will be given you."[1]

We love that story because of its simplicity. At heart, forgiveness is very simple. It can be one of the most difficult things in the world to do, but it's not very complicated. We've used words like release, drop, clear, allow, and now see. It's not doing as much as it is undoing. See this person as someone who did a bad thing and has caused you pain—but as someone who is also needy. In the fable, the man only has to ask for the magic eyes and to want them. There's no great secret to this new way of seeing. You just have to want to.

Ann was nervous about seeing Scott, her ex-husband. It had been four years since he'd left her, two since the divorce was final. Scott was a smooth talker, and she'd once been very much in love with him. A bunch of other women had been, too, and Scott had played the field freely during their decade of marriage. During their marriage, Ann knew about two or three of the affairs. Scott had kept coming back with slick apologies and she'd welcomed him. Since the divorce, Ann had learned there might have been five or six affairs. He was a cad, but a persuasive one. Ann worried a bit that she might succumb to his charms. She felt she was strong enough to avoid a renewed romance with him, but she worried that this meeting might pull her back down the slope.

Still, she needed to see him. She'd become a very different person since he left. No longer in his thrall, she was growing emotionally, spiritually, and professionally. She had a good job, a great church, and a wonderful group of friends. Maybe she was testing herself to see just how strong she'd grown.

The meeting was polite and pleasant. Scott was smooth as ever, but Ann was wary. As he talked about his own life and career, Ann began to see him in an entirely new light. The time for anger was past. Her hatred was slipping away. She saw him as a very sad man, someone desperately searching for himself. She wished she could share what she'd found, the love of friends, the love of God—but he couldn't focus on what she was saying. She watched him walk out into the night and her forgiveness went with him. She was able to release the bad feelings he'd earned. She was able to see with "the magic eyes."

HOW DOES FORGIVENESS WORK?

Now that we've got all the emotional definitions out of the way, let's talk about the nuts and bolts of forgiveness. Exactly how do you go about forgiving someone? What if the other person doesn't want to be forgiven? What if the other person is long gone? What if you need to ask for forgiveness as well as offer it?

People go through a basic process when they forgive, but it varies according to the situation. We can identify four possible situations based on these two questions:

1. Does the person want to be forgiven?
2. Will you have an ongoing relationship with this person?

As we've noted, an "ongoing relationship" doesn't necessarily mean a renewed romance. It may mean sharing custody of children, or continuing to do business together, or seeing the person around town. It might even mean that you remain friends. Those two questions give us a grid (the terms are defined on the following pages):

	WANTS FORGIVENESS	DOESN'T WANT FORGIVENESS
ONGOING RELATIONSHIP	1 • Presentation • Negotiation • Confession • Peace Agreement	2 • Presentation • Refusal • Boundaries • Letting Go
NO ONGOING RELATIONSHIP	3 • Presentation/Confession • Acceptance/"Good Feeling"	4 • Letting Go

1. When the Offender Wants Forgiveness in an Ongoing Relationship

This is the classic scenario, also the easiest. All the other processes are variations on this theme. Perhaps you've had a nasty breakup, but your ex now wants to be friends. Or perhaps, for the good of your children, your former spouse wants to clear the air.

Presentation. Does the other person know what he or she did wrong? People often think they know, but they only have a piece of the complete picture. You need to "present" the situation to them. "I was very hurt when you did that."

It's a good idea to use "I" language in this step. Don't presume to know why the other person acted wrongly, just give your account of things. "I suffered." "I felt bad." "I had a hard time dealing with what you did." You-language ("You couldn't control yourself, so you went chasing after . . .") will provoke a defensive response. Instead, you're at a point where you want to create peace. The other person might know exactly what he or she did—but not how it affected you. Tell your story.

It might also be important to clarify the "ongoing relationship" you have. That's why you're presenting this. "Whenever I drop the kids off at your place, I have these feelings of anger against you, and the children see it. I know I need to let go of these feelings. Could we talk about it?" Or, "I really want to be friends with you again, but there are some issues we have to discuss." This clarification should keep the person from getting a wrong idea about reviving the romance, but it should also make your charges easier to take.

It's tempting to skip over the presentation. "We both know what went on here." But maybe one of you doesn't know. You have to stare the problem in the face before you get rid of it.

Review the gory details, so you're both on the same page.

Randy once tried to make peace with a former girlfriend. He'd made some mistakes in the breakup that had hurt her. They'd had no contact since. Feeling guilty, he wanted to set things right, so he called her and they met for dinner. Somewhat naïvely, Randy asked her to forgive him. At first she was wary, worried that he wanted to get back together. He explained that he just felt bad about what he'd done and he wanted forgiveness.

In the "process of forgiveness," Randy was skipping to confession. But his ex-girlfriend wisely brought it back to presentation. "You really hurt me, you know?" She went on to explain her side of the story. Randy learned a few things, including some new things to be sorry for. He defended himself a bit, clearing up some misinformation she had, but then he apologized again. Eventually she offered her forgiveness.

Even if your offender comes to you, you'll still have to present your case. It's very important that both of you know exactly what's being forgiven.

Negotiation. After the presentation, your offender might plead guilty or not guilty. If he or she doesn't agree with your charges, then skip over to the "Does Not Want Forgiveness" section. If there's total agreement, you can move on to confession. But more likely the person will bicker over some of the details. Maybe, in the time since the event, you've embellished it in your memory. Maybe you've attributed motives that weren't there. Maybe you've tied coincidences together to imagine more problems than really existed. (Maybe that phone number in his pocket really was the dry cleaner, and he only had two affairs, not three.) It's also likely that your ex has forgotten some of the more damning or damaging details.

The negotiation process could be short and sweet, or it could take hours. It's basically a way of agreeing on what happened. Be ready to see a new angle on these events. Some of your bad feelings might dissipate as you understand more from your ex's perspective. But you'll probably end up with a core of bad actions that the other person is sorry for.

What if you were at fault too? Here's where your culpability enters the picture. During negotiations, your ex might raise issues of your own misbehavior. If these are legitimate, be ready to apologize for them. Your goal is to make peace here, and the need for confession can cut both ways. But remember this: Your offenses do not excuse the other person's.

It's sad to see talk shows where such negotiation turns into shouting matches and fistfights. Here's a bit of dialogue that keeps coming up.

"How could you sleep with my sister?"

"Well, you were never there for me—always out at the club or working!"

Maybe both parties are at fault, but the one offense doesn't excuse the other. Both of them need to confess. And we're not saying your issues are talk-show quality, but you might need to offer a confession as well as seek one.

Confession. Once you've agreed on the facts, the guilty party (or parties) needs to confess. Don't be satisfied with "I'm sorry if you were hurt by what happened." The offender needs to say, "I'm sorry for what I did. It was wrong." Lesser apologies might get you through the encounter, but they won't be enough to create a lasting peace in that "ongoing relationship." If the other person truly wants forgiveness, then he or she will work with you in the negotiation process and offer a sincere confession. But it doesn't stop there.

Peace agreement. The final stage of the forgiveness process is some understanding of "how things are going to be now." This is the sort of thing that happens within a marriage when one partner confesses infidelity and the other forgives but requires certain assurances that it won't happen again. The peace agreement might include, say, calling your partner every night while on business trips.

It's a bit different in a broken relationship, but if there's any ongoing contact, you might need to conclude with such a peace agreement. "I'll stop saying nasty things about you." "I'll be nicer about letting you see the children." "Maybe we can be friends now."

2. When the Offender Does Not Want Forgiveness in an Ongoing Relationship

What if you have to keep in touch with this person — because of children, a job, or other social connections — but he or she won't admit doing anything wrong? That's one of the most frustrating situations you can face. How can you forgive someone who doesn't want forgiveness?

Presentation. It's still important to present your issues. Make your charges, but use I-language to make sure you get a hearing. Explain how you were hurt by the other person's actions. Your ex might defend his or her actions, but can't deny your feelings.

Refusal. In this scenario, negotiation takes the form of a not-guilty plea. Your ex doesn't see anything wrong in what he or she did. This will be frustrating for you, but you must not press your case. You'll have to agree to disagree about the amount of blame you can place on this person.

You might be able to wrest some semi-confession from this

conversation: "I didn't mean to hurt you, and I'm sorry it turned out that way." That probably won't satisfy you. Even if the person wasn't being mean, he or she was at least selfish, and that still needs to be forgiven.

Be ready for blame to be thrown back at you. "You made me do that. Whatever I did, you deserved it." You can defuse some of that by being ready to bear a share of the blame—just don't take all of it. If you volunteer a confession for your role in the breakup, perhaps that will inspire your ex to do the same. But if your ex isn't budging, don't cop a plea for the whole crime.

In the same way, you need to be careful for smooth talkers who will make it seem as if they had no choice and that you're just mixed up. Don't let them dissuade you from your main goal: You want to offer a gift of forgiveness, and in so doing, find peace for yourself. Even if the other person doesn't want your gift, you can still give it.

Boundaries. If your ex refuses to confess, then you're forced to make some unilateral decisions. You'll still offer forgiveness (and find your own peace), but you won't be able to reach a "peace agreement" with the other person. Instead, you'll need to decide on your own how to conduct this "ongoing relationship" with the other person. And that might mean putting up some walls—emotionally, if not geographically.

But isn't forgiveness all about tearing down walls? Yes, ideally. But in this frustrating situation where other people won't receive your forgiveness and you have to keep dealing with them, you need to protect yourself. That might mean paring this "ongoing relationship" to the minimum. Maybe you really can't be friends with the person. Maybe you explain that you can't invite your ex inside when he or she drops off the children. Don't be nasty about it, just decide what you need to do to get this frustrating relationship behind you. You got hurt by this person before, and from all indications he or she might willfully do the same thing again if allowed back in your life.

So don't be shy about setting boundaries for your own protection. Forgiveness is a letting go of past problems. It doesn't require setting yourself up for new ones.

Letting go. Now, on your own, you must let go of your bad feelings toward this person. Forgive. Drop the charges. It'd be great if he or she was sorry, but that's not happening. And you can't let your ex hold your emotions hostage any longer. Give up the pain of the past. Stop focusing on it. Allow yourself to think positive thoughts—or at least compassionate thoughts—about your ex. Better yet, avoid thinking about your ex except when necessary. In your ongoing relationship, you'll see each other from time to time, but with appropriate boundaries in place, you can relax. Let go of the hatred and live free.

3. When the Offender Wants Forgiveness, but There Is No Ongoing Relationship

This was the situation when Randy met with his former girlfriend. He wanted release from his guilty feelings, though they hadn't seen each other since the breakup. And you might get a card or call from out of the blue, as your former partner seeks to meet and clear the air.

Or perhaps you're instigating the contact. You've been carrying a grudge for so long that you must present it to the guilty party. You feel you have to say how much you were hurt, and give that person a chance to apologize.

Tom occasionally counsels people who were abused as children.

Though they've severed contact with the abusers, as they go through therapy they feel a compulsion to confront the abuser and present their case. Sometimes such meetings can be very therapeutic, but they're quite dangerous too. The same might be said for encounters with ex-spouses and former romantic partners. Badly done, they can unearth all sorts of negative emotions that might be better left buried.

So, if you're going to confront an old partner that you haven't seen for some time, we urge you to be careful. First, be sure of your motives: Seek peace for yourself, not revenge against the other. Second, be wise in your plans: Can you do this by phone or letter rather than a riskier face-to-face meeting? Third, be clear about the relationship: You don't want to restore the old romance, but do you want to have an active friendship or an inactive one? Finally, be realistic about the outcome: You may not get the kind of resolution you're looking for, and you might just get more frustrated.

Presentation/Confession. In advance, you might want to practice what you'll say. Present your case clearly but humbly. Ask for exactly what you want—a confession. Be willing to negotiate a bit. But be willing to walk away if this isn't working. Don't let yourself get emotionally gripped by this person. It's not an ongoing relationship; you can keep it that way.

If you plan to confess some mistakes you made in the relationship, be clear about that too. Don't get into a tussle over who hurt whom the worst. Your goal is peace.

Acceptance/"Good Feeling." In this part of our grid, we're assuming that the other person wants to be forgiven. So after you make your case, the other person will apologize, you'll accept, and you'll be able to feel good about the past even though there's no ongoing relationship. That's all you came for.

If you're seeking forgiveness, give the person time to digest your confession. You can't expect instant satisfaction. It took you a while to reach this point; your ex might need some time too.

4. When the Offender Does Not Want Forgiveness, and There Is No Ongoing Relationship

What do you do if your ex just left? Gone. Out of your life forever. What can you do?

Basically you have two choices: Continue to live with a heart full of hatred; or release that hatred and start a new life. The first choice, hatred, hurts no one but yourself. Your ex will never feel that, especially if he or she is on another planet. And even if you could communicate that venom, would it do any good? Do you think your ex cares how you feel right now? The second choice is obviously the best choice. Release that hatred. Why wouldn't you?

Well, some are reluctant to do that because their hatred has become such a part of them that they can't imagine life without it. Some feel it wouldn't be honest to say they don't hate anymore when they're sure they always will. Some feel a strong duty to the cause of justice. They don't want to let that scoundrel's crimes go unpunished.

And so they let the injustice continue. They continue to suffer for the wrongs of their former partners. Each day that this grudge consumes them they allow the old relationship to plunder more of their lives.

Letting go. An old phrase says, "Living well is the best revenge." That holds true here. If you insist on taking revenge, then do it by building the best possible life for yourself. We're not talking about fancy cars and bulging bank accounts. We're talking about peace of mind, vibrant new relationships, ways you find contentment and satisfaction in life. Let your life blossom. But you have to let go of the hatred.

That's the wonderful paradox of forgiveness. It seems to be a gift you give others, but its greatest benefit is to you. Forgiveness sets you free.

CLEAN FOR A DAY

Having a hard time forgiving your ex? Try doing it for just one day. On that day, whenever you have a nasty thought about the person who hurt you, say, "I'm not going to let that spoil my day. Save it for tomorrow." At the end of the day, see if your life was better with the forgiveness than it was without it. Then you might want to spend a few more days like that.

REAL LIFE STORIES

KATHIE LEE GIFFORD & EMMA

Kathie Lee Gifford
Kathie Lee Gifford has been described by manager John Blake as "the ideal of what a married woman should be." She and husband Frank seemed to have the perfect marriage, along with two beautiful children, Cody and Cassidy. On her syndicated TV show, Kathie Lee frequently spoke with great enthusiasm of her marital bliss, describing how she and Frank would sit in front of their fireplace and pray and cuddle. It seemed that nothing could shake such a strong bond of love.

That bond, however, was nearly shattered in 1997 when the Globe tabloid revealed that Frank had had an affair with a beautiful flight attendant. Kathie Lee was devastated. She felt totally betrayed by the man she once described to television audiences as "the ideal husband." She strongly considered leaving the marriage, but ultimately chose to stay. That's where the journey toward forgiveness began.

Admittedly angry, Kathie Lee agreed to go to counseling with her husband and also individually. They met with counselor Gary Smalley, a personal friend. She knew that, in spite of her pain, she still loved Frank and their children, and wanted to keep the marriage together. Previously married at a young age, Kathie Lee had no desire to go through another divorce. Forgiveness didn't come easily, however, for such a painful betrayal. Both Frank and Kathie Lee knew it would take time to rebuild the trust that had been lost. Deeply religious, Kathie Lee relied on prayer and Scripture to help her through. Eventually she also came to believe very strongly that her husband had made a one-time mistake and that it was best to look toward their future, not their past. Kathie Lee continued to break down in tears and sometimes anger, however, whenever the subject of Frank would come up on her TV show. It took years before she could talk about the subject of her husband's infidelity with calmness and objectivity.

Forgiveness isn't easy, especially under the media's microscope. When you're hailed as America's "perfect couple," you invite mockery when you struggle. Yet it's apparent that Kathie Lee's forgiveness of Frank has come a long way.

"You expect to be brokenhearted by your enemies, not by the person you trust the most, love the deepest."
— Kathie Lee Gifford

Emma

To her group of single and single-again female friends, Emma seemed to be the luckiest woman they knew. She was the first of the group to get married, and it appeared that she was marrying the perfect man. Joe was handsome, had a good job, came to church with her, got along with her kids—the list of virtues went on and on. They had a beautiful wedding and reception and moved into a lovely home shortly afterward. Everyone was surprised to hear a few months later that Joe's business was not doing well and the two were having some financial difficulties. Surely it would pass soon.

Within two years, Emma was showing up to events without Joe. He wasn't feeling well, she'd explain, or had too much work to do. The truth came out a few weeks later—Joe and Emma were separated. There'd been troubles throughout the marriage, and Joe had finally walked out. Emma was left with a large mortgage payment and many other bills she couldn't possibly pay herself, including loans she'd taken out for the benefit of Joe's failing business. She was in shock and so were her friends.

Eventually Emma won a settlement in which Joe was supposed to pay her back a certain amount monthly toward his loans. This helped somewhat in her struggle to forgive Joe for leaving her in such dire circumstances. But it was still a struggle.

Emma knew there was no hope for their marriage, but for her own peace of mind she needed to work through her anger and bitterness. However, just when she thought she was beginning to reach a level of forgiveness, something would happen to set her back. One time it appeared that Joe had deliberately quit his job so that he wouldn't have to make his monthly payments to her. Forgiveness took a back seat for a while.

There's no happy ending here. Sorry. Emma's still working on it. It's never easy, especially when the person you want to forgive is being difficult. But Emma recently won a battle with cancer and has a new appreciation for the precious gift of life. Life is too short, she realizes, to hold grudges. That's made it a little easier to forgive even Joe.

"Forgive us our trespasses, as we forgive those who trespass against us."

—from "The Lord's Prayer"

6

SELF VIEW

ReStart Principle 6:
Your view of yourself affects how you relate to others.

You can learn a lot about our culture from watching daytime talk shows. We're not guaranteeing that you'll like what you learn. But you will get a fascinating peek at social values in action.

Occasionally you'll see some scantily clad, overly curvaceous woman explaining that once she got her breast implants her self-esteem improved. Now she feels good about herself and that's all that matters. The audience applauds.

What's that about? Has "feeling good about yourself" become our culture's cardinal virtue? Oprah and Montel spend hours of screen time counseling people with low self-esteem. Sally offers them makeovers.

And the audience applauds.

BEYOND THE TRIVIAL
There's a smidgeon of truth in all of this, but it's buried in triviality. The truth is that your view of yourself does affect how you relate to others. A healthy self-understanding will help you

understand those around you. An ancient commandment puts it well: "Love your neighbor as yourself." There's a connection between our treatment of others and our treatment of ourselves.

But what is a "healthy self-understanding"? Does it require cosmetic surgery? Of course not. It's a balanced view of yourself as a valuable person within a community of valuable people. You have rights, but so do the others. You have needs, but so do the others. You're gifted in certain ways, and others have different gifts. You give and you receive. You and others are in balance.

That balanced approach is sadly missing in most of what we hear about self-esteem these days. If you say anything self-critical in public, you're liable to have a gaggle of well-meaning friends clucking away at you, criticizing you for your poor self-image. But we keep seeing people in their talk-show moments of fame, excusing all sorts of relationship crimes by saying, "I had to do what was right for me because, by golly, I'm worth it." And the audience applauds.

The self-esteem craze is a fairly recent phenomenon. Oh, our society had dalliances with self-betterment and positive thinking, but until the 1960s people were taught to see themselves as part of the group. It was important to be a good citizen, a good family member, a good neighbor. Nobody cared much what you thought about yourself. The 60s brought us a "Do Your Own Thing" philosophy, and people don't always realize what a major revolution that was. Suddenly, individuality mattered. You weren't just part of a larger society; you had individual rights.

Pundits called the 1970s "The Me Decade," as the 60s' revolution came to full flower. It was more than platform shoes and disco—it was when the modern self-esteem movement took shape. Books encouraged us to "Look out for number one."

Movies showed us an assortment of characters who faced difficult circumstances but ended up feeling pretty good about themselves.

Social observers kept predicting a swing back to group consciousness. Would the 1980s be "The We Decade"? The 1990s? It never quite happened that way. We remained as stuck on ourselves as ever. In the new millennium, it's safe to say that self-esteem is intricately woven into modern thought.

Does that mean with the "I'm OK, you're OK" feeling that we're all self-actualized and secure in our individuality? No. While people generally agree that self-esteem is a good idea, a host of other factors have conspired to make it difficult for us to be content or satisfied with who we are.

Advertising. The era of ads has advanced to the point that people tune in to the Super Bowl to watch the commercials even if they don't care about the game. And what's the goal of advertising? To make you feel insecure about your present situation. It's true. A deodorant commercial succeeds if it gets you worrying about body odor. Similar things might be said about any number of products. The message of their ads is, "You need this." "You are woefully inadequate without it."

Beauty cult. You might also say we live in an age where beauty reigns. Perhaps it's the growth of TV and movies, which pay a lot of attention to appearance and little attention to anything else. We see beautiful people on screens all the time, and we can't help but bemoan how awful we look compared to them. The truth is, even they don't look that good—what with camera angles, makeup, and cosmetic surgery—but we still feel bad about it. Kids learn this early, especially the girls. "Why would that boy I like look at me when he can watch a Britney Spears video?"

Conspicuous consumption. A booming economy in the

1980s and again in the 1990s brought us to an age of "want it/have it." After a brief fling with "simple living" in the 1960s, it was cool once again to drive an expensive car, live in the biggest house you can't afford, and carry a portfolio of hot stocks. If you didn't have all these goodies, you just weren't making the grade.

Technology. We now have an ever-expanding assortment of toys to buy. Computers have grown faster and smaller. VCRs and CDs and DVDs and HDTV—you must have something with letters in it or you'll be hopelessly out of touch. Of course, this year's must-have gadget will be obsolete in a few weeks, so we're always feeling a bit behind. And even if you can afford all these contraptions, can you ever learn how to use them all? How many of us still have 12:00 flashing on our VCRs?

All of these social developments contribute to our feelings of inadequacy. So while we've learned that it's important to feel good about ourselves, it's getting tougher and tougher to do so. And so, in a strange way, the self-esteem movement itself has hurt our self-esteem. Many of us are like the woman who sat in Tom's office and said, "I know I should have better self-esteem, but I just can't."

We've been talking about society, now let's talk about you. If you've recently gone through a painful breakup, your self-esteem has probably taken a good shot. You might feel rejected by your former partner. He or she might have said some nasty things on the way out—or you might just be assuming things that weren't said. Maybe you're kicking yourself for saying or doing the wrong things. "I just wasn't good enough to keep that relationship together."

Now you've gone through the recovery process, down and back up that slippery slope. Even if you've come to a point of acceptance and forgiveness, you still might feel insecure about yourself. And as you begin to date again, you can't help but wonder, "Am I good enough to get anyone else?"

Our message to you is, first of all, relax! It's normal to feel insecure. Everyone does — especially after going through what you've gone through. You're rebuilding your life right now. You've got some issues, but everyone does. Try to keep a reasonable, balanced view of yourself and others, and you'll be fine.

Look around you at the people you know best. Some of them probably have low self-esteem, right? And others think more positively of themselves. But that's not the whole story. Some of those with low self-esteem are very sweet and giving people, fun to be around. Others are totally fixated on their own shortcomings, and they seem to turn every event, every comment, into a problem for them. Have you noticed this? Of those with high self-esteem, some are friendly and caring — their confidence is infectious. Others are cocky and arrogant, as if the world revolves around them.

So when we say that your view of yourself affects your relationships with others, we're not just talking about your level of self-esteem. There's another factor, something we call self-focus. The question isn't just "How do you feel about yourself?" but "How much do you pay attention to yourself as opposed to others?"

Simple observation shows that some people who think very little of themselves actually think about themselves all the time. Those are the people who are always telling you how incapable they are. You have to be careful not to say anything they can twist into an insult, because they will. Everything is about them. They're incredibly self-focused. We call these people Needers because they need extra attention, extra assurance, extra maintenance.

But other people with low self-esteem don't draw attention to themselves. They quietly go about their business, which is usually serving others in some way. "Don't mind me, I'll just do what I can to help, though it probably won't be much." These are sweet people and great friends, though sometimes you want to grab them by the shoulders and say, "Don't be so hard on yourself." These folks are other-focused, possibly because they don't see much value in themselves. We call them Worshipers because they keep giving honor and glory to others.

Let's look at the high-self-esteem part of the spectrum. There are plenty of arrogant jerks around, people who force everyone else to cater to them. They're legends in their own minds, and completely self-focused. Who cares what anyone else wants or needs? They have their own agenda. We call these people Stars because that's how they see themselves. In group situations, they draw the spotlight to themselves.

But then there are those self-confident people who focus on others. They're aware of their own talents, but they use them to help people. In group situations, they might exercise leadership if needed, but they're interested in what others have to say. We call these people Helpers because that's where their focus is—helping others.

So we have four types of people: Needers, Worshipers, Stars, and Helpers. Do you see yourself in any of those categories? What about your friends? What about your ex? Obviously these are stereotypes. People have different levels of self-esteem and self-focus, and most of us vacillate from time to time. But it might be helpful for you to see where your tendencies lie, and what you can do to improve your situation.

In relationships, we find that Worshipers and Stars get together and Helpers help Needers. It only makes sense. Each has what the other needs. Yet these tend to be unbalanced relation-ships because of imbalances in the individuals involved.

Take the Worshiper and the Star. The Star, with high self-esteem and high self-focus, loves to receive the worship of the Worshiper. The whole relationship is about the Star. Of course the Worshiper doesn't mind because he or she has low self-esteem and a strong other-focus. The Worshiper doesn't want any attention. Some couples function pretty well like this for many years, but if the Worshiper grows in self-esteem or self-focus, he or she might get upset at the lopsided quality of this relationship. This has occurred with many classic "housewives," who loyally serve their Star husbands until they realize that they have value too. Then there's conflict, as the relationship struggles to find a new equi-librium. Some couples can't make this adjustment and split up.

The Helper-Needer relationship has a similar imbalance. The Helper, with high self-esteem but a strong other-focus, tries to meet the many needs of the Needer. The relationship is all about the Needer. The Helper doesn't mind because he or she finds sat-isfaction in helping, especially this beloved one. But at some point the Helper might burn out—maybe the Needer needs more than the Helper can give. The Helper suddenly realizes that his or her own needs haven't been met. This is the classic situation of the addict with the co-dependent partner who seems addicted to help-ing the addict. The non-stop giving actually creates an "enabling" situation that does nothing to change the low self-esteem or high self-focus of the Needer.

Maybe you've been in a relationship like one of these. Or you might be about to enter a new relationship with these charac-teristics. We've talked with many people, following divorce, who are temporarily Needers. Their self-esteem has taken a major hit and yet they're very focused on their own pain and recovery. They gravitate toward Helpers. It's wonderful to have someone meeting your needs, but a Helper-Needer relationship can stunt your growth. Seriously, you need to grow into a healthier self-esteem and a healthy balance of self-focus and other-focus. But a Helper-Needer relationship is based on the Needer's need. If the Needer stops being so needy, the relationship stops working. That's one reason we strongly discourage rebound romances. Even if you find the ideal person to help you through your recovery, that relationship might hurt your recovery, or your recovery might hurt the relationship.

We've also seen some people who are other-focused after a divorce. These Worshipers tend to fall for self-possessed Stars. When you've been treated like dirt by an ex-partner you now consider to be pond scum, you enjoy having a new partner who is strong and confident and doesn't mind having you around. Stars don't even have to pay much attention to Worshipers—just let them tag along. Of course these relationships are dangerous too. Many healing hearts are used and abused (intentionally or not) by these self-focused Stars.

So, is there any hope of a healthy relationship for you? Sure. But you have to get yourself to the center of the spectrum: balanced self-esteem, balanced focus. If you're not there yet, be careful about entering any new relationship. Even if it meets your needs temporarily, it won't satisfy you in the long run. As you become more balanced in your own self-esteem and focus, the relationship will go out of alignment.

Randy once had an old guitar with a broken key. The keys are those six knobs at the top that tighten the strings, keeping them in tune. He couldn't get it fixed right away, so in the meantime he just tuned all the other strings to that one string. As that string went flat, he tuned the whole guitar flat. Because he was playing by himself, he could get away with this. The chords sounded fine because the guitar was in tune with itself, and only a listener with perfect pitch would be able to sense a problem. When he eventually fixed the key, he tuned that single string to the correct pitch. He strummed a simple chord and winced. Of course all the other strings had to be retuned too.

That's how it goes when your view of yourself is out of balance. You gather people around you who will tune their strings to yours. But when you finally get tuned up, they need to change as well.

There's another potential problem with entering relationships when your view of yourself is out of whack. It goes back to that curvaceous woman on the talk show. There's something wrong with the idea of changing your look in order to get self-esteem. The audience applauds her gutsy decision to go after what she wants, but what kind of self-esteem is she really getting? Obviously, it's appearance-based. She feels good because she looks good. But what will happen to her as she ages? Will she have to go through a succession of facelifts and tummy tucks to keep feeling good about herself? Some people have gone down that road. They've been tightened so much that they raise their eyebrows to pull up their socks. But there's actually something very sad about reaching outside of yourself for that extra thing that will give you the self-esteem you don't have inside yourself—whether you're reaching for a new look or a new relationship.

We've seen many Worshipers and Needers who try to find their self-esteem in a new partner. "I must be okay if I'm good enough to get this partner." They prance around with their new lovers on their arms and they feel great about themselves. Some people seek to establish their worth by gaining a plurality of partners. "Look at all these people who want me!" But that's a minefield. As long as you're reaching for self-esteem outside yourself, you won't find lasting satisfaction. If you get dumped by your new lover(s), you're right back where you started.

A healthy view of self starts with your basic identity as a human being. Atop that intrinsic value, pile up all your particular gifts and abilities, your interests, your passions, and your experiences. And your faults. You're a unique person of value, worth getting to know, even with your problems — especially with your problems. Every so often a student will write a nicely crafted play or short story with one fatal flaw: The characters are too perfect. Problems make people interesting, so don't ignore yours. It's all part of the glorious mixture of who you are. But you don't have to depend on other people or on external sources such as beauty or money for your personal worth. You carry it within you.

So how do you get there? How do you develop healthy self-esteem if you don't have it? You can read all sorts of books that say great things about you, but they quickly become like cheerleaders at a game your team is losing badly — a little too perky and totally unconnected with reality. You need more than pep talks. You need a plan. Here's ours:

- Identify the villains.
- Renounce their messages.
- Create a supportive environment.
- Adjust your focus.
- Forget about it.

Identify the Villains

There are reasons for your lack of confidence. Maybe you know what these are, maybe not. Maybe your mom always told you that you'd never amount to anything. Maybe you forgot your lines in your third-grade class play. And quite probably your breakup left you feeling inadequate, incapable of succeeding in relationships, or even feeling deeply guilty.

As most of us go through life, we hear voices. This doesn't qualify us for the asylum; it's just part of normal life. These voices are memories of comments from our upbringing, interpretations of modern events, and some of the common self-talk we engage in. Sometimes these voices begin whispering our faults, reminding us of our failures, teasing us about our foibles.

"You'll never succeed at this."

"You're making a fool of yourself."

"You look terrible."

Practically everyone hears these voices. Your level of self-esteem depends on how much you believe them. Your level of self-focus depends on how much you pay attention to them. Well-balanced people who hear the voices say, "Oh, those are just the old voices again," and then turn up the stereo. That is, they get so involved in real life that they don't have time to obsess about the voices. They also realize that the voices tell lies.

Sometimes in court, lawyers will call character witnesses to testify about the kind of person the defendant is. "He's a rotten guy, your honor. When he was young, he kicked a dog. What kind of person would do that?"

The defense attorney then has the task of challenging the testimony, separating fact from opinion, perhaps even impeaching the witness. "Did you actually see him kick the dog? Wasn't he in fact playing with the dog? And weren't you just jealous because you didn't have a dog? Your honor, I move that we throw this testimony out!"

All right, so it's not exactly "Law and Order," but it's similar to the process you need to go through when rebuilding your self-esteem. Those inner voices are character witnesses, testifying to all sorts of negative qualities that you supposedly possess. You need to hear them out, but then interrogate them. Is this testimony fact or fiction? Is it just an assumption based on a partial story? Is it based on some emotional response of the past that has nothing to do with who you are now? Be scrupulously legal in your analysis. If an accusation is ten percent true, isolate that ten percent and throw the rest out. But if it's all bunk, then impeach the witness and toss the testimony out of court.

Let's consider where some of these false witnesses come from.

Growing up. This is such an obvious point that it's often overlooked. Most of us grow up feeling smaller, dumber, and weaker than everyone else—because we are. A five-year-old boy is not going to be as good at most tasks as is his older brother. A twelve-year-old girl isn't going to get the attention from boys that her teenage friend down the block gets. Children are clumsy, ignorant, and irresponsible compared to older children and adults. And so, as we grow, we feel a lot of rejection. Some people carry that into adulthood. Their voices replay messages from childhood, applying them to the present day, implying that the person is just as clumsy, ignorant, or irresponsible now.

Teasing and competition. Most of us quickly learn to compare ourselves with children our own age. That competition can be fierce. It's amazing how thoroughly kids keep track of the rankings. Randy still remembers being the fourth best kickball player in fourth grade.

Children's identities get formulated around their rank in the group. Star athlete, smart kid, artistic prodigy, tallest in the class. But woe to the fat kid, the slow kid, the late bloomer, the ones picked last for the team. Despite all the reassurance of parents and teachers, they know they don't have as much perceived value in the class as others. And kids can be brutal in their teasing. There is some adult somewhere who is convinced he or she is no good, all because the second-grade bully called him or her "Stinky."

Parental expectations. Some parents expect too much of their kids. There are some fathers who run their homes like boot camp, some mothers who raise their children to be President. But even more reasonable parents will sometimes set the bar a bit too high. That might not always be so bad—that's how kids grow. But childhood failures can get imprinted on our hearts, unless parents are exceptional at encouragement. Of course, some parents blatantly bash a child's self-esteem because they wanted a boy instead of a girl, or because Junior isn't the athlete that his older brother is. But even good parents can say things that get posted on your emotional bulletin board for you to review for years afterward.

Misunderstandings. Aunt Sadie tells ten-year-old Jennifer, "Ooooh, you look so big in that dress." As Sadie smothers her niece in an embrace, she can't see that the girl is scowling. Jennifer's already the tallest girl in her class, and she's developing faster than the other girls. She's worried about looking fat. Aunt Sadie was trying to say that Jennifer was looking grown-up. But because of Jen's juvenile anxieties, she took a compliment as an insult. That can happen in a lot of ways, especially to those who are self-focused. Passing comments are taken as criticism.

Religion. We'll tread lightly here because we believe in the value of religious faith. But many people learn a kind of self-loathing from their religious training. Guilt becomes a major factor in one's faith. God is so good, they believe, and I'm so rotten. God requires perfection, and we humans are incapable of doing anything right. Without delving too much into theology, let us say that this approach is only half-true. Any religion that honors God as the Creator must have some respect for humans as God's creations, even the pinnacle of his creation. And certainly the Christian tradition, along with some others, holds that God loves human beings. That's the whole point of the "John 3:16" verse that gets waved around at football games. Yes, human beings are fallible, but we're also valuable. Both those truths need to be kept in balance. And Jesus himself affirmed such a balanced approach when he quoted the command from the Hebrew Scriptures: "Love your neighbor as yourself."

STONE SOBER

A rabbi has said, "A man should carry two stones in his pocket. On one should be inscribed, 'I am but dust and ashes.' On the other, 'For my sake was the world created.' And he should use each stone as he needs it."[2]

That's exactly the balanced approach we're talking about. It does us no good to pretend we're perfect, yet we have great value to the Creator.

Renounce Their Messages

Once you've identified some sources of your bad feelings about yourself, you need to disagree with what they're saying about you. Hear the testimony of those character witnesses, but then debunk them. It's not easy. You may have gone for years believing what those voices have said to you, but now it's time to say no to them.

Some people actually talk to themselves. In public, this might earn you some funny looks. But in your solitary moments, why not? Say, "That's not true!" when those voices are defaming your character. Some people develop a little saying that sums up the self-image they want to have, something like "I am a beautiful person created and loved by God." Then they repeat that phrase when attacked by self-doubt. That's not such a bad idea.

We're intrigued by the "act as if" approach some counselors have been using lately. If you are convinced you'll fail at some project and are afraid to try it, act as if you are confident in your abilities and see what happens. You don't actually have to be confident, just pretend you are. You'll probably find far more success than you expect. That'll shut up those voices for a while.

The major problem in debunking those voices is that they're usually half-right. It would be fairly easy to renounce those nagging doubts if they were always completely false. "You're too short to amount to anything" isn't going to bother a guy who's six-foot-five (unless he wants to be a power forward in the NBA). But it might bother the guy who's five-foot-five. In renouncing that voice, he needs to cut through the reasoning. "Yes, I'm short, but that doesn't mean anything. It's silly to think that my size would keep me from doing anything I want to do (except playing power forward in the NBA)." Those voices in your head are great at twisting logic. You have to straighten it out.

Divide what you have done from what's been done to you. If people have done hurtful things to you, that's not your fault. Stop feeling guilty for being victimized. Even as you look at your breakup, there are probably some things that you did wrong. But you need to hold your ex responsible for the things he or she did too. Not that you need to hold a grudge—we discussed that in the last chapter. But don't take all the blame on yourself. The same holds true for formational events in your childhood or adolescence. Sure you've made mistakes, but some things just weren't your fault.

Divide who you are from what you have done. After that first step, you're still left feeling bad about some things you've done. It wasn't all your fault, but you can take some of the blame. Maybe you're ashamed of things you've done. But the truth is that we've all acted wrongly at times. We've done ignorant, perhaps even hurtful things. But we learn. We grow. Through time we become different people. We don't need to be defined by the deeds we have done. Just because you've failed doesn't mean you're a failure.

Divide who you have been from what you will be. As you honestly appraise your past, maybe there's more stuff you don't like than stuff you do like. Maybe you just don't like the self-portrait that emerges, even after you've done the first two steps of dividing. Maybe you do seem like a failure or a scoundrel. Fair enough. But sometimes you just have to draw a line in the sand. That was then, this is now. The future can be far better than the past.

Create a Supportive Environment

In a normal day, how many supportive messages do you get? Not just "Hi, how are you?" but genuine affirmation of who you are or what you're doing. Does your boss praise your work? Do family members or friends express their admiration?

In the same day, how many destructive messages do you get? How many encounters do you have that criticize your ability or value? Add in any media messages that make you think, *I wish I looked that good,* or, *Are my teeth too yellow?*

You'll probably find that you have several times more negative feedback than positive. If that's true, then your self-esteem-building project will need to reverse that. Can you make changes in your environment to make it more supportive?

Friends. You would expect friends to offer a lot of positive feedback. Many do, sometimes just by being there for you. But sometimes friends can get in the habit of mocking each other. Men can try to one-up one another with insults. Women can turn catty in some situations. And suddenly you find yourself feeling awful among the people you should feel good with.

So talk about it! Say, "I'm going through a rough time right now with my self-esteem, and some of these joking comments hurt. I really need your support right now." Good friends will respond to that. If they don't, start looking for some new friends. (And you might try talking first with one close friend, so you have that person's support when you discuss it with a larger group.)

Remember too that the best way to get support is to give it. You might take a friendship to a deeper level by asking about someone else's problems and worries.

Media. We don't need to say much more about this except to be careful about what input you get from TV, movies, music, and magazines. Most of us don't filter these messages very well and the result can be destructive. You might want to cancel a subscription to a fashion magazine because it presents an impossible image of womanhood. You might want to stop watching "Dawson's Creek" because it makes you feel old. You choose what messages you want to get.

Your job. You might not have much choice here, but see what you can do. Is your boss always criticizing you? What would happen if you asked for gentler treatment? Would your self-esteem improve if you had lesser responsibilities, or greater ones? If those options are impossible, could you team up with coworkers to provide mutual support? Or do you need to look for a new job? (Don't make that jump unless you have to. Job-hunting can also take a toll on your self-esteem. Even if you get a better job situation, the process of finding it can be grueling. Prepare yourself emotionally for such a move.)

Projects and hobbies. Many people find relief from bad jobs in great hobbies. Then again, some hobbies can grow frustrating. If golf has stopped being fun for you, try bowling. Try to find some project that will stretch you a little without overwhelming you. Take a photography class if you've always wanted to. Write that novel that's been brewing in your head (or at least a chapter of it). You want to get a sense of victory from a pursuit well done.

Your inner monologue. Keep talking to yourself in positive ways. Renounce those negative messages as they arise and offer yourself support as you need it.

Adjust Your Focus

We've been talking mostly so far about the self-esteem side of our equation. But you might find it easier to move first toward a balance between self-focus and other-focus. If you find yourself obsessing about your lack of self-worth, focus on helping others. Volunteer for a tutoring or mentoring program, or just help out in a local charity or church. Groups like that are always looking for helpers and the requirements usually aren't too stringent. You'll find yourself doing something valuable for others, which will boost your own sense of worth.

If you're a Worshiper, focusing on others and ignoring yourself, you need to tilt the balance the other way. You're probably already volunteering for half a dozen organizations. If you're running yourself ragged with service projects, perhaps you should cut back. But even if you maintain your current obligations, throw in something you do for yourself once in a while. Eat some ice cream. Take a bubble bath. Rent a video once a week and pop some popcorn. Could you set up one night a month as "Me Night"? It won't be easy, but force yourself to say no to everything else and do something for yourself. (You might need a friend to check up on you to make sure you do it.) Over time, you might begin to look forward to that one night. It's certainly a nice step toward balance. You'll still be heavily committed to others—nothing wrong with that—but you'll be more aware of your own needs as well.

Forget About It

The best thing you can do about self-esteem is to forget about it. If it's a problem for you, it keeps cropping up. Those voices keep harping on every flaw. That's why you need to do some of the things we've suggested—identifying the villains, renouncing their messages, creating a supportive environment, and adjusting your focus. But after you take those steps, don't keep tinkering. Don't keep lifting the lid of the pot to see if your new, improved self-image is simmering yet. Just relax.

If you can go a week, or even a day, without thinking about your self-esteem, that's a victory. (Of course you can't plan not to think about something. Just relax. Go about your business and let the growing occur.)

IF YOU'RE A STAR OR A HELPER

The point of this chapter is that your view of yourself affects your relationships with others, and that's true whether your self-esteem is high or low. We've already discussed the dangerous relationships that Stars and Helpers tend to get into with Worshipers and Needers. But what can they do to improve their chances in relationships?

If you're a Star. Remember that a Star is both self-confident and self-focused. So our advice to you is simple: Grow up. We're not being disrespectful. We're just pointing out that children start out with a strong self-focus that expands as they grow. The infant's world is all about its own needs. Then Mommy and Daddy enter the picture as need-meeters. Toddlers start to explore their world, but still with a strong focus on their own needs. Only later do most children begin to be aware of how others are feeling. But some grow into adulthood without really developing that knack. Maybe that's your story.

The growing up we're talking about is a matter of expanding your focus. Cognitively, you have to decide that other people matter at least as much as you do. Then you have to remind yourself regularly to put this decision into action. Put yourself in the skin of someone else. Try to see what they're seeing.

It could be helpful to work with a friend who's bold enough to tell you the truth. If you start acting selfishly, you need to know it. You might also get involved in some small group of people who will care for you but also challenge you. It will help you to see yourself as part of a team.

If you're a Helper. Again, this is someone who is self-confidently focused on others. The danger in relationships for this person is burnout. You can't meet all the needs you want to (as your self-esteem keeps telling you that you should be able to). You might push yourself too hard.

But your relationships will suffer too. They'll tend to be one-way. All the energy will flow from you to the other person, as you play messiah. That can be tough for you to maintain. But it's also debilitating for the other person, who has little incentive to become anything but a Needer.

You need to know your limits. You can't do everything for everybody. Learn to say no to some needs that will stretch you too far.

You should also make it a point to get more in touch with your own needs. You're so focused on others that you probably haven't thought much about what you need. But you really ought to let others serve you once in a while. Get to know some other Helpers and talk together about your own needs, then take turns helping one another.

As you seek to build a new life after a breakup, your view of yourself is one of the major stones in your foundation. If that's out of balance, you won't be able to build anything durable on top of it.

REAL LIFE STORIES
➤ OPRAH WINFREY & CYNTHIA

Oprah Winfrey

One of the most admired and respected women in America today, Oprah Winfrey made it to the top in a profession that had few successful black women. Today her name is a household word. Yet Oprah came from a childhood that was very different from her current life of fame and fortune. Born illegitimate to a mother who left her to be raised by relatives, she grew up dirt poor. At an early age she was raped by an uncle, resulting in a miscarriage. Drifting from relationship to relationship as a teenager, Oprah tried to find the stability she lacked at home, but she was never satisfied. At age fourteen she was sent to live with her father and stepmother, who insisted that she settle down, make good grades, and stop running around with boys. Oprah credits them with saving her life.

Oprah's career in broadcasting started in Baltimore with a show called "People Are Talking." This was also the period of Oprah's first intense love affair, which lasted four years. The only problem was that the man was married and had no intention of leaving his wife. Oprah was having problems with her weight, as she would throughout her life, and, according to friends, her self-esteem was at an all-time low. When the relationship broke off, she actually considered suicide. She was only twenty-seven. As she recovered from her depression over the failed relationship, she began to see a correlation between her overeating, low self-esteem, and destructive relationships. In order to have a healthy relationship with a man, she realized, she first needed to love herself more, no matter what her current weight.

In 1986 Stedman Graham Jr., a handsome ex-basketball player with a master's degree in education, began asking Oprah for dates. She refused his invitations at first. Despite her resolve to view herself as an attractive, desirable woman, Oprah had difficulty understanding why this very attractive man wanted to get involved with her. Eventually, however, she relented and they entered into a long-standing relationship. A relationship as public as theirs hasn't been without its problems, but it appears to be permanent. Oprah has finally realized that, no matter what her appearance or financial status, she deserves to be loved by a wonderful partner.

> *"Mr. Right is coming, only he must be in Africa, and he's walking."*
>
> —Oprah Winfrey

Cynthia

Cynthia was caught in a bad marriage to a controlling, abusive man. He wouldn't let her out of the house without permission. He wanted dinner on the table when he arrived home, and he punished her when he didn't get what he wanted. He belittled her in public and private, convincing her that she was useless without him. Sometimes he hit her.

Why did she stay with him? She bought his lies. Day after day he told her that she was no good, that she'd never amount to anything on her own, that she was lucky to have a man like him to take care of her. This confirmed what she already thought about herself.

The seeds of her poor self-image had been planted early. Her father had left her mother when Cynthia was quite young. The girl was raised with the "help" of an uncle, who abused her sexually. Cynthia tried to tell her mother, but she didn't get through. Her mom didn't want to know or didn't want to admit knowing. The uncle was very nice to help out as he did, the mother kept saying. Cynthia figured it must be her own fault—she thought she must have deserved it.

So as an adult, she got involved with men who told her the "truth" about herself, that she was worthless. She wouldn't trust men who flattered her. But the abusers fit right into her life, and she finally married one.

Then Jan moved into the neighborhood and started coming over. Cynthia kept her guard up, but Jan befriended her anyway. They'd go out shopping, out to the movies, and out to a church group Jan was part of. From Jan, and from that group, Cynthia gained support she had never known before. She began to see herself as a person of worth. Yes, she had something to offer, no matter what her husband said. As she grew stronger, she began to stand up to her husband more. Sensing that he was losing his hold on her, he became even more abusive. One day, after he had hit her, she summoned the strength to leave him.

How could she function without him? Cynthia wasn't sure at first, but she slowly learned that she could. With the support of her friends, she built a life for herself. She still had bouts of self-doubt, but she had a new assurance. After several years, she met a wonderful man—the complimentary kind of guy she used to ignore—and she married him. They had a beautiful baby girl.

Happy ending, right? Well, this story takes an unhappy turn. A traffic accident with a drunk driver left Cynthia badly injured and her husband dead. A major crisis like this would send most people careening back down the slippery slope. If Cynthia gave back all her hard-won self-esteem, you couldn't really blame her. Maybe she really did deserve to be miserable. It'd be easy for her to see life that way.

But she didn't. She grieved deeply for her lost husband, and she struggled to raise her daughter on her own. But she never sank back into self-blame. She now had a network of friends to support her. And the person who helped her most during this recovery was her mother—the one who had turned a blind eye to that childhood abuse. Cynthia had made peace with her, offering forgiveness, and now she was receiving proper maternal care.

Cynthia has faced far more than her share of hardship, but amazingly, through all her struggles she has learned to love herself.

7

KEEPING COMPANY

RESTART PRINCIPLE 7:
Your healing can be helped or hurt by the company you keep.

SCOTT was twenty-five, living with his mother and a younger sister, bouncing around from job to job. He was quite intelligent, but a strong strain of Attention Deficit Disorder kept him from committing to college or a steady career. Though he was a very pleasant young man, he felt insecure socially. His ADD led him to say inappropriate things from time to time, and a facial birthmark marred his physical appearance, so he often found it easier to keep to himself.

But Scott had a great group of friends—some high school buddies he had kept in touch with, and a few of their pals. They'd all go out bowling or dining or to the movies. In summer they played softball every week. When Scott was unreasonably antisocial, some of the guys would literally drag him out of bed to join them.

Then Scott's mom passed away. She had been a source of strength for him throughout his difficult childhood, and now she was gone. Of course it's a tragedy when anyone's parent dies, but this was even worse because Scott had needed her so much.

That's where Scott's friends came in. They didn't just go to the funeral and send flowers. They practically adopted Scott over the next few months. They stepped up their social schedule, making sure Scott often had things to do, but they also seemed sensitive to Scott's grief. If he really needed to be alone, they'd let him, but they wouldn't let him drown in his misery. When Scott's sister was taken in by an aunt and the house was sold, some of Scott's pals even let him move into their apartment.

With such a cadre of supportive friends, Scott was able to heal from the grief of losing his mother. They gave him a new start. In the next couple of years, he got a steady job, began taking computer courses at night, and eventually moved into his own apartment. That's the effect good friends can have.

Linda was growing impatient with her husband, Rob. He'd been jobless far too long, and showed no desire to start working. They'd bought a house together back when both of them were gainfully employed, but now the mortgage payments were taking most of her salary, and their savings account was dwindling. Why didn't he get busy?

A couple of times he'd started new jobs, but quickly found them distasteful, and soon he was back home again. Linda loved him, but what could she do? She encouraged him and prodded him. She begged and cajoled. She screamed and threatened. But nothing seemed to work. Then she moved out.

Her friend Patty took her in. Patty had an extra room at her place and invited Linda to stay as long as she needed to, to get things sorted out with Rob. Linda had no idea how things would turn out. Was this the beginning of the end of their marriage? Or would this bold move shake some sense into Rob? She kept meeting with him from time to time, but she held firm on her demands. She wouldn't come back unless he got a job or got counseling. He had to make some changes.

After these meetings, she would come back to Patty's place emotionally wrecked. She loved the guy—and she was determined to make their marriage work—but she was sure it wouldn't work unless he took action. And if he wanted to sink in self-pity, she wouldn't sink with him. She'd plop herself down on Patty's easy chair and unload her latest frustrations, and Patty would listen. Sometimes Patty would reason things out with her. When Linda began to cave in, Patty would give her strength.

Eventually Rob did make some changes, and Linda finally moved back in with him. They're continuing to work through some tough issues, but they're moving slowly forward. They're making a new start, and they both have Patty to thank for it.

Good Friend, Bad Friend

Your healing can be helped or hurt by the company you keep. Friends like Patty or Scott's buddies can speed you along the path of recovery. But with other sorts of friends, your journey can be seriously delayed.

After getting dumped by her boyfriend, Barry, a young woman named Teresa found consolation from the other women in her office. They agreed that Barry was an ignorant jerk, that she was too good for him, and that if there was any justice in the world he would die a prolonged, painful death. It became a wry joke at the office: The trash cans were nicknamed Barry's Place; the paper shredder was Barry's Destiny, and when they heard a toilet flush they'd say, "Barry's calling!"

The women started taking Teresa out with them after work,

bar-hopping. They'd gripe about the men who'd been in their lives and tease any new men that approached them in these bars. "Love 'em and leave 'em," they told Teresa. "Yeah, leave them before they leave you."

At first, Teresa felt welcomed and supported. These women seconded her feelings of anger and bolstered her self-confidence. But soon she realized that they were just a bunch of bitter victims who'd never fully healed from their broken relationships. They were stuck in their own anger and depression. Now they saw men as the enemy, and sex as a weapon. Teresa didn't want to go that way.

She began to skip their after-hours bar sessions. Instead, she'd go home and cook for herself, or read, or chat with her sister on the phone. She missed the frantic energy of the office gang, but she was glad to be free of their bitterness. At home, by herself, Teresa began to assemble a new attitude. She could love herself without hating men. The women at work sensed her pulling away from them, and they turned their bitterness against her. She began to be snubbed at coffee breaks and lunches. Soon she was looking for another job.

Friends You Don't Need

Just as great friends can aid your recovery, the wrong friends can sabotage it. Let's look at seven types of friends you don't need during this time, and then seven friends you do.

The Emotional Trigger. It's not their fault, but some people will simply remind you of your pain. The most common examples of this are your ex's family. We've talked to many divorced people who terribly miss their in-laws, but they can't deal with the reminders involved in seeing them. Temporarily, you might need to avoid such people. If you've gotten along great with your in-laws, you might want to drop them a note explaining that you still care for them but, given the situation, it's best to stay away from them for a while. They'll understand.

Some divorced people find it difficult to be with couples they used to hang out with as a couple. Those friends are still friendly, but their very "coupleness" reminds you that you're no longer in that category. If that's a problem for you, spend more of your time with single friends.

The Judge. Some folks think they're helping you by evaluating everything you did wrong in your relationship. They play amateur shrink, trying to help you learn from your mistakes. Surely you can benefit from their wise advice!

Well, probably not. At this point you're well aware of mistakes you've made, and you'll be unearthing more in the future. You don't need pontification; you need peace. Avoid these judges if you can. Unfortunately, you can't always avoid them entirely. They might be your parents. They could be other relatives or bosses or co-workers—people who assume they have earned the right to critique you. If you can't stay away from their judgments, try to shield yourself from them. Let their comments roll off you. Smile and thank these judges for their "helpful" comments, and then ignore them. If you think they might be saying something worthwhile that you're just not ready for, write it down on a sticky note and paste it on your calendar for a year from now. Maybe it will be more helpful then.

The Doomsayer. Teresa found herself embraced by a pack of doomsayers—the women at work. At first they seemed encouraging and supportive, but soon she learned that they were miserable and planned to stay that way. In fact, they were feeding off of her misery. Misery loves company. When she showed signs of breaking free from their misery, they shunned her.

As you begin to share your pain with others, you'll find yourself invited to many pity parties. Women love to complain about men, and men love to complain about women. Jilted people love to share their tales of woe, often over drinks. "Life is a pile of pain," they say. "Relationships are impossible. We're all doomed to be lonely." When your experience confirms their thesis, they'll welcome you into their world and buy you a drink. "Tell us how bad things are for you."

And when you're first nursing your hurt, when you feel abandoned in your sorrow, it's wonderful to find people who commiserate. Someone understands me! But as you grow, you leave the doomsayers behind. Or they keep pulling you back.

What you need more than anything right now is hope. You need to have a vision of a brighter future. You might be sloshing around on the slippery slope right now, but you know there's healing ahead. That's the hope that the doomsayers are bent on destroying.

The Substitute. How many times has this happened? An old friend introduces you to her second husband, and he's a spitting image of her first. It doesn't happen all the time, but it's fairly common. It's like a soap opera suddenly inserting a new actor into an established role. The character has been created; it's just a different body playing the part.

We're not just talking about appearance, though it sometimes happens like that. Substitutes can exhibit inner traits that you used to enjoy in your ex. You might find them confident, or empathetic, or brilliant, or artsy—perfect to assume the role that's already been written into your personal drama.

Substitutes are extremely tempting. You've just had an agonizing breakup with someone you used to love, and here's someone else who's just like that person without all the bad stuff. Well, the truth is you don't know the Substitute well enough to see the bad stuff yet. And the problem is that you think you do.

When a Substitute reminds you of your former partner, you assume that he or she is just like your old flame in many ways. The new relationship starts at Square Two, as you apply a lot of your old history to this new fling. So you and the Substitute zoom forward, basically picking up where you and your ex left off (before all the bad stuff), and it feels wonderful . . . for a while. But such relationships are doomed because they have a false foundation. Eventually, you'll learn that the Substitute has bad stuff too. You'll find that your assumptions are faulty. Sooner or later, your Substitute will resent being treated like someone else.

We've already discussed the dangers of rebound relationships. You can nip these in the bud if you recognize Substitutes before you get involved with them.

The Rusher. We spent a whole chapter on the importance of time in the healing process. You can't rush things. Healing won't happen overnight. Rushers are those dear people all around you who just don't get it. They think a breakup is like the flu—it knocks you out for a week and then you're back in the game. Or maybe divorce is like a broken arm—you're in a cast for six weeks, tops. And so they start prodding you to get better when they think you've been down long enough. What's the matter with you? You've been moping around for three months already!

Somewhere, deep down, they want what's best for you, but the truth is that they're tired of commiserating. You've reached the end of their sympathy, and now it's your turn to care for them for a while. Or so they think.

The sports world is full of scandals involving coaches and trainers who rush injured athletes back into action too soon, causing even worse injuries. Young gymnasts are hurried back into training for the Olympics. College football stars have been shot up with cortisone and sent back out to play when they ought to take more time for healing. In Philadelphia, one well-known hockey player charged that team trainers downplayed the seriousness of his multiple concussions in order to get him back on the ice in time for the playoffs. The first game back, he was hit hard and went down—bam, another concussion. Now no one knows if he'll ever play again.

Teams have just begun to understand that it's in their own best interest to allow players time to heal. "Rehab" is a word you didn't see much in the sports pages twenty years ago. Now it's common for players to take time for rehabilitation. People are starting to grasp the idea that effective healing requires time—and probably more time than you want to give it.

Try to convey that to the Rushers in your life. Get them thinking about your recovery in terms of years rather than weeks. And if they don't get it, stop listening to them. Don't let them rush you. And if they start to resent you for taking "so long" to get better, avoid them. You don't need that kind of pressure.

The User. Users have a kind of radar that zeroes in on hurting hearts. They know your self-esteem is low, and they can rather easily make you dependent on them. Then they can enjoy a relationship that's seriously tilted in their favor. They might use you for sex or money or status or just for kicks. In any case, they'll do serious damage before they're through.

Joe was such a user. Renee met him as she was recovering from a broken engagement, and he seemed to meet all her needs. Her self-esteem had hit rock-bottom, but Joe made her feel important again. They shared a love of theater, and he had a dream of starting his own theater company—if only he had the money. Renee wasn't rich, but she had credit cards, and she was delighted to be able to back such an ambitious project, led by such a wonderful visionary. Charging thousands of dollars on her cards, Joe began his project. There were a few minor performances in small venues.

Meanwhile, Renee was growing more attached to Joe. Though she had always been a good Christian girl, Joe was demanding more of her sexually. How could she refuse? He was everything to her. She told herself it was okay because she would someday marry him. But soon she learned that he was also sleeping with some of the actresses he auditioned for his company. Joe kept going off on "theater trips," charging hotel rooms and expensive dinners on Renee's credit cards. When she challenged him, he'd find ways to challenge her self-esteem. He knew the right buttons to push.

Despite Renee's best efforts, the theater company was falling apart. Actors weren't getting paid, and Renee began getting calls from club owners who had pre-paid for performances that weren't happening. Joe stopped calling.

Renee was left feeling ashamed, abused, and seriously in debt. She had hoped Joe would save her from the misery of a previous breakup, but he was a User (and a scoundrel) and he just made everything worse.

The Caretaker. But Users aren't always so dastardly. Sometimes they can be well-intentioned people who get their kicks from rescuing those in need. That sounds great, doesn't it? If you're in need, that's just what you're looking for, isn't it? A rescuer? A savior? Someone to take care of you? Well, not exactly. You need support, but you need to rescue yourself. You need to grow. A savior will make you dependent again. Rescuers actually stunt your emotional growth. Caretakers keep you from taking care of yourself.

Relationships with caretakers aren't always romantic, either. A caretaker might be a friend who views you as a project. At first you welcome the support, but soon you realize that the focus isn't on your need, but on the caretaker's ability to meet your need. Often a caretaker will get jealous if you get your needs met elsewhere, or alarmed if you show signs of independence.

Caretakers can help a lot in the short term. Accept their help, but don't let them keep you dependent. They're similar to Users, actually, except they're using you to fulfill their desire to do good. Because of that, you can use these users for a while. Just don't get used by them.

Friends You Need

For every negative, there's a positive. You'll meet plenty of Users, Judges, Rushers, and the others during your recovery. But thankfully, there are other friends who are truly helpful. These are the people you should seek out and spend more time with.

The Caregiver. Obviously you need some quality care during your recovery. You need a listening ear, embracing arms, words of encouragement. The Caretaker offers those, but in a selfish way. The Caregiver focuses on you and your needs. Caregivers aren't threatened if you get help from others. They truly want whatever's best for you. And when you start to get better, they ease themselves out of the picture. Oh, they'll always be great friends, but they won't try to keep you needy. They'll rejoice with you as you take those solid steps toward independence.

The Needer. This might surprise you, but as you begin to step toward renewed health, it helps to have people who need help from you. Maybe they're a step or two behind you on the journey. Along the way, you can say, "I've been there. I know what you're going through. Here's how I took that step."

Education experts have found that some children learn best from "near-peers" rather than their teachers. Near-peers are slightly older students who share what they just recently learned. So the sixth-grader can teach the fourth-grader about fractions. While the sixth-grader doesn't know all the educational methods that the professional teacher might employ, the experience of learning fractions is still rather fresh in her mind, and she can convey how she learned it. The fourth-grader is inspired by the example of the near-peer. If she learned it, I can learn it too.

The same principle applies in recovering from a breakup. A struggler could read a hundred books like this one, but he would benefit even more if you would come alongside and say, "Just a year ago, I was exactly where you are. Let me tell you what I discovered." You help the Needer, but you also gain a great deal yourself. It has to be a great boost to your self-esteem to realize that you have something to offer another person, and the process of helping has drawn you out of yourself.

Just be sure you act as a Caregiver and not a Caretaker. Be sure your primary motives are genuinely altruistic. You should be mostly interested in giving help, not taking an opportunity to bolster yourself.

And make sure your Needer isn't a User. They're fairly easy to distinguish because the User tries to gain control, preying on your need. But if your Needer begins using manipulation, keep your distance. Don't get drawn into a situation of dependence, on either side.

One other note: You probably won't have much help to offer for at least the first six months of your recovery. Give yourself time to take a couple of steps along the pathway, then look back and see if there's someone you can help.

The Co-Struggler. You need to develop friendships with people who are on the slippery slope with you. Compare notes. The Co-struggler is not behind you on the path, but right beside you. You aren't just offering help; you're both helping each other.

Psychologists have long espoused the principle of group therapy. Many clients find this absurd, thinking, *I hired you to give me your professional insight. I don't want to pool my ignorance with a bunch of other troubled souls.* But those troubled souls might have valuable personal insights into what you're going through. And you can feel a bit more normal as you see other people having the same difficulties that you're having as you climb the slope.

Tom has long been involved with a divorce-recovery organization called Fresh Start, and he often speaks at its seminars. The comment he keeps hearing is this: "The workshops were great and I learned a lot. But the most important thing was just meeting all those other people who were exactly where I was. I thought I was all alone. I thought I was a freak. But suddenly I was with a group that thought I was normal."

You can go to a seminar or group therapy or just establish friendships with Co-strugglers around you. But you need that kind of mutually supportive relationship. If you have too many Rushers in your life, you'll think you're hopelessly behind schedule, that you're terminally heartbroken. But gather some Co-strugglers alongside you and you'll realize that you're doing just fine.

The Model. Right now, you might be conjuring up images of Elle Macpherson (or Marcus Schenkenberg) and saying, "I wouldn't mind developing a relationship with a model." Sorry. We're not talking about that kind of model. We're talking about someone you can model your life after, someone who's a bit ahead of you on the pathway.

This is your near-peer. Just as you reach back to help the Needer, the Model reaches back to help you. Try to find someone who had a similar breakup about a year before yours, but make sure they've been recovering properly. (Teresa might have thought the women in her office could be models because several had been divorced. But it turned out they hadn't recovered much at all.)

You might approach the Model with questions about your struggles. Most strugglers love the opportunity to give advice about things they've successfully struggled through. Be honest about your problems and ask them to be honest about theirs.

Be careful, however, about becoming too attached to the Model emotionally. If you get romantically involved, the Model could easily become a Substitute—someone who has the qualities you're looking for, but someone who'd be disastrous for your recovery. It's probably best to seek Models of your own gender. Even then, avoid growing too dependent on the Model. Learn from the person and grow, but avoid any manipulation or jealousy.

The Visionary. An ancient proverb says, "Without vision, the people perish." You might say the same thing about your journey toward wholeness. You need a vision of the future, the light at the end of the tunnel, the firm footing at the top of that slippery slope. You will be healthy again, in another year or two or three. You will be confident again. You'll be able to watch old movies without bursting into tears. You might even be able to enter another romantic relationship.

You need Visionaries to remind you of that. Maybe these are people who have struggled up the slope and found wholeness of their own. Look for people five to seven years removed from a painful breakup. They can tell you, "Things used to look bleak for me too, but look at me now. I lived to tell about it."

Tom has served this role for a number of people as he has told his story of divorce and recovery. There was a time when he thought he'd lost all that mattered, but miraculously his life has turned out pretty well. If it can happen to him, it can happen to you. That's why we keep telling you these "real life stories." Recovery is happening all around you, and it's in your future too.

So surround yourself with visionaries who feel like they've been to hell and back. Or maybe they're just cheerful souls who live their lives with a sense of optimism. If they can bring you hope, grab onto them as friends and don't let go.

Doomsayers rob you of hope, but visionaries provide it.

The Prophet. Nowadays when you say prophet, people think of the annual New Year's predictions in the *National Enquirer*. Will Pamela Anderson elope with a Saudi prince? That's not what we mean. You don't need to start hanging around people who fore-tell the future.

But do hang around those who tell the truth. Not foretellers, but forthtellers—people who speak forth a message you need to hear, whether you want to hear it or not. Back in Bible times, that was the prophets' job description. The forecasting was a side-effect. Their main task was to deliver a message of truth from God to kings and commoners alike. And so Nathan stood before King David and said, in essence, "You have sinned with Bathsheba." Surely the king could have pulled out the old slingshot and silenced this prophet more easily than he'd nailed Goliath. But he knew he needed to hear that truth, no matter how embarrassing it was.

We all need to hear unpleasant truths from time to time.

If you're getting into a rebound relationship, you need a prophetic friend to say, "Stop! You're heading for disaster."

If you are turning to alcohol or drugs to mask your pain, you need to be told, "That's not going to help anything."

If you let your anger seep out into your relationships with family and friends, you need one of those friends to stand up and say, "Whoa! You're punishing me for what your ex did! If you keep alienating the people who love you, you'll be even worse off."

If you sink into a terminal bitterness, you need a wise pal to say, "Enough already! Wake up and smell the flowers."

But wouldn't a Judge say the same things? We already told you to avoid Judges. How is a Prophet any different?

A lot of it has to do with pride and humility. The Judge knows what is best for you, or assumes so. The Prophet is just delivering a message. The Judge assumes that he or she has earned a right to be heard, when the Prophet actually has. The Judge imposes a point of view upon you—in the Judge's opinion, this is how you should live. The Prophet urges you to make a choice based on your best interests. That's why the Prophet's forthtelling of truth often sounds like foretelling: "If you keep doing this, then this will happen. Is that what you want?"

Make no mistake, Prophets can make you mad. They know just the thing to say to jolt you out of complacency. Or if you're rising high on some false hope, they won't hesitate to burst your balloon and bring you back to earth. There'll be times when you're tempted to turn your back on a Prophet and run the other direction. But you need these people in your life.

The Jester. Sometimes you just have to laugh. You need people around you who make you happy. Things can get very dismal in your life. You need people who can raise your spirits, reminding you of the good stuff. This doesn't have to be a joke teller. It could be a friend who simply has a sweet spirit and a positive outlook.

Riding home from a disappointing softball game, some team members were grousing about the missed opportunities, the botched plays, the bad calls. Then one of them said, "Look at that sky. Isn't that phenomenal?" And it was. All orange and purple, as the sun was setting amid a thin fabric of clouds. Suddenly the game didn't matter that much.

Sometimes you need someone to do that for you. You need someone to point out a brilliant sky, to play you a beautiful song, to bring you fresh flowers, to remind you that every moment you live and breathe you are a miracle.

Emotional Triggers, through no fault of their own, remind you of your pain. You need some Jesters to remind you of the joys in life.

Company Not to Keep	Issue Involved	Company to Keep
Emotional Trigger	*What you think about*	Jester
Judge	*The correction you need*	Prophet
Doomsayer	*How you see the future*	Visionary
Substitute	*How you are changing*	Model
Rusher	*Pace of healing*	Co-Struggler
User	*How you help others*	Needer
Caretaker	*The care you need*	Caregiver

How to Connect

Now you know what kind of people you want to have around you, but how do you make that happen? We recognize that most people with shattered confidence lose a bit in their social skills, so it might not be easy to assemble the dream team of friends we just recommended. But here's an assortment of guidelines and ideas that might get you started.

What do you have? Make a list of the ten people closest to you. Then go through and mark the friends you need and friends you don't. If you can identify any of those ten friends or relatives with our descriptions (User, Model, Jester, and so forth) then write that description beside their name. For right now, put an X beside the names with negative descriptions (Friends You Don't Need), and forget about them. Circle the names with positive descriptions (Friends You Need).

The names you've circled belong to people already in your life who can help you. Spend more time with these people. Right now, plan a way to connect more with one of these people in the next week. You can deepen your friendships with others in the coming weeks, but start with just one.

What do you need? Now go back over our list of seven Friends You Need and make a note of any who don't appear on your list of closest friends. Do you have a Co-Struggler on your list yet? A Visionary?

Reread our discussion of these roles and try to think of other people you know who fit these descriptions. Maybe they're not close friends, but acquaintances, coworkers, or friends of friends. If you come up with any, choose one that you think you could get to know better. Plan a way to begin that process in the next week.

What don't you need? Go back to those Xs on your list. This is tricky. You probably won't be able to avoid these people entirely, nor should you in all cases. You might find ways to lessen your interaction with them, especially if you strongly feel that they're impeding your recovery. But at least be aware of their negative influence upon you and try to shield yourself from it. You might always have a Judge in your life, for example, but you don't always have to pay attention to the judgment.

As you look over those Xs, plan any ways that you could decrease their effect on you in the next week or two.

Groupthink. When it comes to making new friends, think in terms of groups. It's very hard to befriend new individuals, especially if your confidence is low, but there's safety in numbers. Group events allow you to interact casually with a number of people. That in itself can be a valuable confidence-builder. Individual relationships can quickly grow intense, subject to pressure and misunderstandings. But you can ease yourself into a group, becoming part of the interaction without feeling too threatened.

Institutionalize. Where do you find groups to get involved in? Look for institutions such as churches, synagogues, the Y, local charities, arts groups, civic organizations, businesses. The institutional backing of these groups also provides some security. If it's just "a bunch of fun folks getting together at Mary's to watch videos"—well, you never know what that might turn out to be. A cult? An orgy? A family reunion? But an institutional event has some accountability.

Strugglers Anonymous. Especially if you need Co-Strugglers, Needers, and Models in your life, look for groups of people that are going through similar problems. A local counselor might have a therapy group you could join. If that seems a bit too clinical for you, look for divorce-recovery groups in churches or synagogues. (Some singles groups would also fill the bill, but others are essentially dating services.) The AA people have it right: It's important to connect with people who are going through what you're going through. If you'd be interested in attending a divorce-recovery seminar, we're involved with an outfit called Fresh Start. Call 1-888-FRESH-START to see if there's a seminar scheduled for your area.

Follow your bliss. A friend of ours, speaker Tom Jones, makes this suggestion: Think about the kind of person you want to be, then look for places where you can find people like that. As you identify your own passions and interests, you can often find groups that share those. Do you want to become more artistic? Then join a theater group or arts club or take a class that will improve your skills. Do you want to be an athletic person? Then look for ski trips and hiking expeditions or join a volleyball league or bowling team. Do you want to be more spiritually minded? Then get involved in a church or synagogue or spiritual discussion group.

Family matters. Chances are, you'll find your greatest support or your worst hindrances within your own family. Maybe both. You probably had some family members on your list of ten, and you probably circled some names and Xed others. It's especially tricky to deepen some relationships while avoiding others within the same family. But your family matters. These are the people who know you best—or think they do. They've earned the right to counsel you—or they think they have. A supportive family can make your recovery a stroll in the park, but a difficult family can make it a barefoot walk on broken glass.

Communicate with your family members as best you can about your agenda for recovery. Educate them about the time it might take you to work through this and the stages you need to negotiate (perhaps by giving them this book). Ask them for the kind of help you need from them. Warn them when you're going through especially tough times.

If that doesn't work, and if your family insists on making your recovery difficult, you'll need to withdraw from them as much as possible. Plan to make peace with them at some future point, but for a few years now, you simply may need to be free from their influence.

If you do that, or if your family is already distant (or non-existent), you'll need to create your own family. Through the connections you make in the various groups mentioned above, or within your natural social circles (or even your business), collect a handful of people who can "be "family" for one another. Within that group, dine together, play together, celebrate one another's birthdays. Create for one another a place to belong.

If you can't pull together a family of friends, consider asking an existing family you know well to "adopt" you. Explain what you're going through and the kind of support you're looking for. If you're young and estranged from your own parents, think about asking an elderly or middle-aged couple with an "empty nest" to sort of fill in as your parents. You can provide them with some love and joy as you receive a sense of belonging.

Same gender. Apart from families and groups, let's talk about individual relationships. As you look for people to fill the roles we discussed earlier, look especially among your own gender. You'll be strongly tempted to enter a rebound relationship, and you'll want to protect yourself as much as possible. Need-meeting relationships can become pretty intense quickly, and you don't want to add any romantic fuel to that fire.

No romance. If you ignore that advice, please follow this. You might find an opposite-sex friend who meets particular needs during your recovery. You might have late-night conversations and private dinners as you pour out your soul. But you need to make a rule: No romance. Talk about it explicitly in advance, just in case. "I don't know if there'd ever be any danger of this, but we need to say it from the outset: We will not get romantically involved with each other. We will care for each other as friends. Okay?"

If you find yourself moving in that direction, at least give yourself a time period—say, two years. "We can't become romantically involved until June 15, 2004, okay? No matter how special this relationship becomes, we will not touch romantically or even kiss until then. That's the rule. It just wouldn't be a healthy relationship. After that, who knows?"

Boundaries. Even in a non-romantic, same-gender friendship, you need to observe reasonable boundaries. Often these need-meeting relationships flash quickly and burn out fast, causing pain on top of pain. If you find a kindred spirit, don't throw yourself at that person. Don't meet every night. Don't call at 3 in the morning. Don't spend every waking hour chatting with him or her online. You don't want to foster dependency in yourself or the other person.

For that reason, we recommend finding several different people for support. Build your Dream Team of Jesters, Prophets, Visionaries, and so on, and develop reasonable supportive relationships with them all.

REAL LIFE STORIES

⌐--→RONALD REAGAN & AL

Ronald Reagan

It was the perfect Hollywood marriage. Two rising film stars—Ronald Reagan and Jane Wyman—wed on January 26, 1940. They'd met on the set of "Brother Rat" shortly after Wyman had filed for divorce from her first husband. They seemed to have it all—fame, good looks, the Hollywood social scene. In reality, however, they had very little in common. Wyman opposed Reagan's burgeoning interest in politics. She was a worrier, and he was much more of an optimist. Eight years and two children later, the marriage ended in divorce, with Wyman keeping custody of the children.

Reagan was deeply hurt by the divorce. For the next few years he struggled with feelings of failure. Hollywood isn't a great place to heal. If you're going through a crisis of confidence, there are plenty of people who will eagerly drag you further down. But then Reagan met Nancy Davis. Though she was also an actress, Nancy was very different from Jane Wyman. Rather than dismissing Reagan's political ideas, she listened to him and urged him on.

Eventually, four years after his split from Wyman, Reagan married Nancy Davis. He'd learned that it was important to have a marriage partner with similar interests. And Nancy became his closest partner, not only in romance but also in his career. Knowing the importance of "the company you keep," Nancy always made sure he was surrounded by people who were supportive of him and his dreams. Years later, after he was elected president, if people on Reagan's staff did not seem to be wholeheartedly on his side, Nancy Reagan would see to it that they were removed.

Reagan once said that coming home to Nancy reminded him of stepping out of the cold into a warm room with a fireplace. This "comfort zone" undoubtedly had a great influence on Reagan's life and career. He was apparently well aware of her contributions, and often turned to her for advice—both personal and professional. He must have recognized qualities in their marriage that were missing in his first marriage. He and Nancy were on the same track, with the same goals.

Nancy Reagan's protectiveness of her husband is a model that wouldn't work for every marriage. However, it's unlikely that Ronald Reagan would have achieved his phenomenal success without the support of a wife with just this trait. Ronald Reagan realized that Nancy was not only his life-partner, but also his greatest supporter.

> *"Honey, I forgot to duck."*
> —Ronald Reagan to wife Nancy
> after being shot in 1981

Al

After ten years of marriage, Al's wife finally had enough of his constant drinking, and filed for divorce. It was a bitter blow for Al, and in the next few years he spiraled even further downward, drinking more and more. His only friends were the ones at the bars he frequented. At least they commiserated with him in his bitterness and anger toward his ex-wife, and they never nagged him to stop drinking.

Then Al's physical health started to deteriorate badly. One weekend, afraid for his life, Al checked himself into a rehab center instead of going to a bar. He came out a month later, sober and with a schedule of AA meetings to attend.

The next weekend, Al felt at loose ends for something to do with his time and decided to drop in and visit his old friends at the bar, even though he had no intention of drinking. Al did well in his resolve not to drink, but it was all too easy to fall back into the habit of complaining about his ex-wife. He continued to visit the bars each weekend, and amazingly he wouldn't drink, just complain. Of course he continued to be bitter and depressed about his divorce. He wondered why being sober didn't help him feel any better emotionally.

Finally, an acquaintance from Alcoholics Anonymous started talking with Al about the "higher power" mentioned in the first of AA's Twelve Steps. He invited Al to attend a church service with him, and for the first time Al heard a message about God that made sense to him. In the church, he also met a whole new group of people who were friendly and interested in him and invited him to come back. In addition, Al discovered that the church had a support group for divorced people.

Al had finally found a safe place to begin his healing. Controlling his alcoholism was an important step, but as long as he kept company with the same group of negative people, his recovery couldn't proceed. Once he was in the company of people who encouraged his recovery, rather than supporting his negative attitude, he was free to move ahead.

8

HELPING
OTHERS

RESTART PRINCIPLE 8:
*You complete your new start by
helping others.*

WHEN life gives you lemons . . .

You might be tired of that saying, since it's been bandied about
by people who look like they've never suffered anything worse than
occasional heartburn.

When life gives you lemons . . .

We know! We don't want to be trite here, but there's an important lesson to squeeze out of this cliché.

When life gives you lemons . . .

So maybe squeeze wasn't the best word to use there, but we
think we have a few insights that might make this hackneyed slo-
gan a bit more ap-peeling.

When life gives you lemons . . . (all together now) . . . make
lemonade!

You probably know some people who seem to have cartloads
of lemons. They've suffered greatly, and they haven't done anything
with their suffering. They're stuck in one of the stages, probably
anger or depression. As a result, they're sour. They moan about

everything. They have ways of turning any good news into bad news. You try to cheer them up, and they bark at you. You come away from a meeting with one of these people with a bad taste in your mouth.

But others seem to be far too sugary. They don't want to think about any bad things because that might ruin their complexion. These folks are so nice and cheery, you just want to punch them in the nose. And it's not just that they maintain a bright spirit for themselves; they run around dousing everyone else with their sugar water. They insist on sewing silver linings into all your clouds. People like this seem to have no concept of suffering. Maybe they've just been lucky in life, or maybe they're stuck in denial.

Two extremes. Neither one works by itself. Take a swig of lemon juice, or down a glass of sugar water — either one will make you sick. But put the two together and suddenly you have a refreshing beverage.

You need lemons in your life. Otherwise it's sickeningly sweet. The lemons life gives you — the lemons life throws at you — these put flavor in your drink. They build character. Way back in the first century, one writer reminded suffering souls, "Consider it pure joy . . . whenever you face trials of many kinds, because you know that the testing of your faith develops perseverance. Perseverance must finish its work so that you may be mature and complete, not lacking anything."[3]

And you might know a few people who have successfully combined the lemons of life with the sugar of faithful perseverance. You can tell that they've gone through a lot, but they're not bitter. They seem "mature and complete, not lacking anything."

Here's the beauty part. People like that can reach out to help others who are suffering. In the midst of your pain, the last person you want to see is one of those sugary messengers telling you to "turn your frown upside down." You feel like saying, "I'll turn you upside down if you don't shut up!" You want advice from people who have been where you are. You want them to take your problems seriously, not shrug them off with a "Don't worry, be happy." Those who have been through the wars are uniquely equipped to help those in the trenches.

And that act of helping others brings a sense of closure to the helper's own suffering. No, it doesn't solve everything, but it provides some meaning to that person's life. As you help others, you'll find a kind of redemption that completes your own healing process.

So when life gives you lemons, serve lemonade. Don't just make it, don't just drink it, but prepare a big pitcher of the stuff and see who needs some.

SECURITY AND SIGNIFICANCE

Psychologists have asserted that there are two basic human needs: security and significance. Needing food, clothing, shelter—those are security needs. Desiring achievement, art, religion—that's significance. Wanting healthy relationships—well, those needs would be a bit of both.

Certainly our relationships offer a form of security. The TV phenomenon "Survivor" showed us people forming alliances to keep from getting voted off the island. Alliances make us strong, whether they're international treaties, political maneuvering, TV-show finagling, or marriages. Partners protect each other. Families provide for their members' physical needs.

But relationships also give us a sense of significance. People take pride in their family name. Joe is not only Joe, but the husband of Susan. Parents see their combined DNA taking shape in their children, and they pass their morals and wisdom to succeeding generations.

Our young friend Manny recently complained that his life was in total upheaval. Why? A romantic breakup? No, on the contrary. He had a girlfriend. It was the first serious romance he'd ever had. Suddenly everything mattered. He couldn't be so laid back about his work, his free time, or his future plans because he mattered to her. Manny was an artist, and a good one, but suddenly his art had greater significance to it. He wasn't just splashing colors around—he was building a life, one that included his girlfriend.

Now we realize it's dangerous to talk about security and significance to those who have suffered painful breakups. We don't want to open old wounds. But you need to understand what exactly you have lost, and how you can get it back.

If relationships bring us both security and significance, breakups steal them away. In some cases of divorce, the security issues are huge. Who gets the house? Who gets the money? The standard of living that the couple has struggled to attain is suddenly axed in half. Divorce settlements are intended to provide for the financial security of the lower-earning spouse and children. But it doesn't always work that way. And apart from dollars and sense, there are issues of personal security. Who will care for me when I am old? Will I ever be loved again?

Breakups also threaten our significance. Do I matter to anyone anymore? Significance involves a sense of purpose. Some people find it in their careers, but relationships also provide a rich source of purposeful living. Are you investing your life in anyone else's life? In coming generations, will anyone remember you?

One brokenhearted man told us, "I used to buy flowers for my girlfriend all the time. I loved to show her that she was loved. Since we broke up, it's hard to get used to not buying flowers. I'll pass a flower shop, and instinctively want to stop in and buy something. But for who? For what? The flowers have no purpose any more. It's very depressing."

We're not trying to get you depressed with all this talk of security and significance. We just want you to realize that you might have lost some very basic things. Even after you've struggled up the slippery slope, you might still be hurting for security and significance. The good news is that you can regain these things by reinvesting your life in others—not in new romances, but in healthy friendships.

You can find new security by entering mutually supportive relationships with others. We've already talked about the importance of family, whether it's your own relatives or a new "family" you create. You need to gather people around you who'll show love and receive love—not because of a person's loveliness, but simply through mutual commitment. Be on the lookout for needy people, people who have suffered losses as you have. Keep bringing these people into your family. The best way to be loved is to show love. And the best way to restore your lost sense of security is to be part of a group of loving people.

You can find new significance in the same way, by reaching out to people in need. Just like love, significance is circular. As you show others that they're important to you, they feel more significant. That generally improves their situation and makes you feel important for helping them. Throw a boomerang by giving others a sense of significance, and it will come right back to you.

After the wounds you've suffered, that might be exactly what you need.

THE SIGNIFICANCE OF SUFFERING

Shortly after graduating from college, Randy experienced a painful breakup. He ended one dating relationship to pursue another, but the new girlfriend decided she wanted to "just be friends" and by then the old girlfriend was long gone. Randy spent about a year kicking himself for the choices he'd made and scolding God for letting him make those choices.

Then he got a call from his buddy George. It seems George was about to call it quits with his girlfriend because he was interested in someone new. Did Randy have any advice? Did he ever! Randy told George his own story, being completely honest about his mistakes and their outcomes. George was grateful for the guidance.

And as Randy hung up the phone, it occurred to him that he'd just written the last page of that chapter of his life. He felt a sense of completion. For a year he'd been wondering why—why he was so stupid, why the second woman appeared in his life at that vulnerable moment, why she teased and left him, why God let it all turn out that way—and now he had a small answer. Maybe all of that had happened to keep George from doing the same dumb thing.

That's a minor example of a major idea. Since his time in a Nazi concentration camp, Victor Frankl has long dealt with that why question. It was essential, he discovered, for victims to find some reason for their suffering. It didn't really matter whether the reason was right or wrong, good or bad. They just had to have a sense of purpose to the whole thing. He called his approach logotherapy, from the Greek word *logos,* meaning reason or meaning.

Your own experience probably falls somewhere between Randy's youthful dalliances and Victor Frankl's horrific woes. You've suffered, and even after your emotions get put back together you might still ask the question "why?" Was there a purpose in what happened to me? You might find the answer as you help others. Without his own painful lesson, Randy would've had nothing to say to George. And without your far more serious pain, you wouldn't be equipped to help other needy souls. But now those experiences are on your résumé, and you have something to share.

WHAT DO YOU HAVE TO OFFER?

Many people shy away from helping others because they're convinced they have nothing to offer anyone else. They still feel beaten down by their own experiences, and they doubt that they have anything anyone else wants. We've already discussed the damage a breakup can do to your self-esteem. When you're convinced you belong on the discount shelf in the dollar store, you don't expect anyone else to value your support very much.

You're selling yourself short.

That's not just a pep talk. We did all that self-esteem-building stuff a few chapters ago. We're saying that your status as a wounded, insecure struggler is the perfect credential for the job of helping others. The perfectly confident person whose biggest struggle each day is what to have for breakfast—how can that person help anybody who's hurting?

When you sell your house, you want a realtor who's sold a lot of homes. When you get laser surgery done on your eyes, you want a doctor who has done hundreds of these operations. And when you're struggling emotionally, you want help from someone who has had deep, emotional struggles.

Think back to your darkest times. Who was most helpful to you? Chances are, it was someone with some experience in the struggling business.

Now, toward the end of your healing process, you're on the other side of that equation. You've struggled, and while you don't have all the answers, you have the wisdom etched by experience and a heart made soft with pain. You might find it hard to believe, but other still-suffering people need exactly what you have to offer.

"I'm not very smart," Tina said. "I dropped out of school and I've had a number of bad relationships. I know I need to build my self-confidence by doing things for others, but I really don't think there's anything I can do."

Tom had just given his final talk at a Fresh Start seminar, encouraging people to complete their new start by helping others. During the discussion time, Tina was opening up. "Everything I've tried I've failed at. No one could look to me as a leader or role model. I have nothing in my life to offer anyone."

Maybe you know how Tina felt. We've met many people with those feelings, or variations on them, though few have put them as clearly as Tina did. When he first heard her comments, Tom was thrown. What do you say to someone who's so sure of her inadequacy? "Obviously you have no clue how capable you are"? No, but Tom didn't know her, and he had no basis on which to boost her ego.

But then he flashed back to a moment in his own recovery. It was a time when his self-esteem was abysmal. He had no idea what he was going to do with his life. What could he do? But Tom had a friend who worked at a school for mentally retarded children, and Tom would occasionally stop by and play basketball. At first he was just killing time, but he began to notice how much the kids appreciated him. He wasn't doing anything! He was just shooting hoops and playing a few other simple games with these disadvantaged kids, but they made him feel ten feet tall. When he arrived, their faces broke into wide smiles, and he could tell they enjoyed having him around. It was an incredibly affirming experience, one that helped him rebuild his hurting self-image.

It might be hackneyed to say those kids gave Tom more than he ever gave them, but he knows it's true. All he gave them was himself. He took whatever he was and put it on their basketball court, and they gave him their love and appreciation. In the process, they gave Tom his life back.

With this experience in mind, Tom responded to Tina's query. "Have you ever thought about working with the disabled or the mentally retarded?"

Tina seemed surprised at first. "I can't believe you said that! I have a younger brother with Down's syndrome. I never really thought about working with mentally challenged people, but that might be a good idea."

As the seminar went on, Tina kept mulling over specific things she could do. It was as if Tom had opened a door for her and she was thinking her way through it. Before the meeting was over, she announced to Tom that the next month she'd volunteer to help with a Special Olympics program her brother was in. Extremely grateful, Tina said she thought this advice would change her life. "I've been in therapy for four years, but you've just answered a question that I've been struggling with all that time."

Maybe that's an overstatement, but it's an interesting comment. And it illustrates the importance of this eighth ReStart Principle. Therapy usually digs for what's inside you. Nothing wrong with that. We have already suggested that you "identify the villains" that have hurt your self-esteem and "renounce their messages." That's inner work, and it's quite valuable. But it's incomplete if you never take that final growth step—reaching out to others. Our guess is that Tina, in her four years of therapy, got into a vicious cycle. She understood her lack of self-esteem very well, perhaps too well, but that didn't change anything. She still felt bad about herself, and she felt bad about feeling bad. But reaching out to others can break that cycle. It's not about you or your feelings anymore.

Tom never did learn what happened with Tina and the Special Olympics, but he can guess that her experience was similar to his. When you help people, especially very needy people, you end up with strong evidence of your personal worth. Because you're not focusing on your own feelings, those new positive feelings can sneak up on you, get past your defenses, and change your whole outlook.

Renewed self-esteem isn't the only payoff of serving others. You also gain more of a sense of control. This is especially important if you were more of a victim in your breakup. You've had an extended period when things have been happening to you, and you've had little say in them. Not only the initial breakup, but also that roller-coaster ride up the slippery slope. You never knew what emotion was coming next. But as you begin to help others, you begin to take control of your life again. You choose to do something positive, and the choice itself is a positive step.

There's also a kind of redemption when you invest your life in helping others. While your new experiences can never undo the old pain, they can create something of value beside it. In the midst of the Special Olympics, Tina might be able to say, "This wonderful thing I'm doing would never have happened if I didn't hit bottom after my divorce." That's not to say that the good activity makes everything all better. You'll still bear certain emotional scars. But it does give you a sense of wholeness. You've traded in your old life for a new one.

Let's say you've driven a sports car for several years. You've driven around the country in it, visiting a lot of cool places. But then the car started acting up. It was always in the shop, it seemed, and when you got it back there were still problems. One day you were driving on a winding road and the steering failed. You wrapped that sports car around a tree. It was totaled, and so were you. Well, almost. A lengthy hospital stay got you patched up and when you got home there was an insurance check waiting for you. Now you've just bought a new vehicle—maybe not another sports car. Let's say a sport utility vehicle—and you are enjoying the drive. It's a different kind of drive, but it's good.

Are you tracking with this extended metaphor? The sports car was your old relationship, which, to put it bluntly, got wrapped around a tree, sending you into a period of recovery. Don't think of the SUV as a new romance, but as all the things you're doing now—your new life. Now, as you're driving the SUV, you're still allowed to think wistfully of the good times you had in the sports car. And you're still going to wince a bit over the memories of the accident and the long convalescence. There wasn't anything good about all of that . . . except that you wouldn't be tooling around in this great new SUV if it weren't for the accident. You wouldn't want to go through it again, but the new vehicle provides a bit of comfort, a bit of redemption.

"I wouldn't wish what I've gone through on my worst enemies," Tom has often said, "but I wish my closest friends could learn what I've learned." The pain doesn't get erased, but it gets transformed. And you get transformed—into a wiser, more compassionate person who helps those in need.

WHAT DO PEOPLE NEED?

We can almost hear you shaking your head. Wiser? More compassionate? Transformed? I wish! Unfortunately I'm still the same old klutz who got into this trouble to begin with. What could I possibly give anyone else?

We heard a cute story from a missionary woman who was translating the Bible into the language of an Amazon tribe. She and her teammate, another middle-aged woman, were meeting every day with a man from the tribe in order to learn the language. He was very helpful. But like the other men of his tribe, he wore no clothes. Maybe just a vine around his waist. The women were grateful for his help, but his nakedness was somewhat distracting. On their next trip to the main mission station, they sorted through a thrift shop that was there, and they found some Bermuda shorts. These were a hideous color of green with a gaudy lime-green belt, but they'd do the job. At their next meeting with the man, they proudly presented him with this gift, "for all the faithful service he had rendered." He was very touched and excited, promising to wear this gift the next day.

Sure enough, the next day he came to the front of their hut and called out to them. "Come, see. I'm wearing what you gave me!" They rushed to the door and looked. He was wearing the lime-green belt. Just the belt.

The point is that when we give gifts to people, we don't always know what they appreciate most. Wrap up a new plaything for your cat, and it's likely to go crazy over the wrapping paper. Share your "wisdom" with a suffering friend, and he or she might just be glad you're taking the time to talk. We can go to great lengths to give people what we think they need, but often they appreciate something else. And when we fear we have nothing to offer, we get thanked for just being there. Sometimes presence is more important than presents.

So let's take a look at what suffering people really need. We want to offer them life-changing ideas, plans for reconstructing their lives, advice that makes everything clear. But the best assistance comes in other ways.

They need someone to be there. You know how lonely suffering can be. You think you're forgotten—that no one cares. What a delight it is to have someone spend time with you! You've been there, and now you're on the other side. Hang out with people in need. You don't necessarily have to do anything or say anything. Just be there.

From time to time, we've visited elderly friends and relatives in nursing homes. At first, it's a frustrating experience, especially if they're not very talkative. You feel you have to fill the silence, to entertain them, to bring some excitement into their drab lives. But eventually you realize that silence is fine. They don't need entertainment or excitement; they just need you. They need to see you, feel your presence, smell you. You can just sit and watch Wheel of Fortune with them. They merely need to know that you consider them worthy of a few minutes of your time.

They need a listening ear. You remember what this was like too. You're so full of random emotions that you need to let them out. You have to get them out on the table and sort through them. You need someone to help you with that process.

Now you're the helper. Others need you to hear their troubles. Listen to them. Maybe it's a niece who's slogging through the third grade. Maybe it's a brother who lost his job. Maybe it's a friend from church who just received a frightening diagnosis.

Fight off the urge to give advice. Most people can see their own way out if you'll help them listen to themselves. Try to listen actively. Ask questions. Clarify points you don't quite get. Follow their logic. You don't need to have all the answers for people if you ask the right questions.

They need acceptance without judgment. You know the guilt that goes along with suffering. Sometimes it's religious guilt: Divorce is a blot on your permanent record; or perhaps there's sexual activity you're ashamed of. Sometimes it's just the shame of being an obviously imperfect person when everyone else is pretending to be perfect. "Sorry to ruin your party by being so sad. Don't let my bad mood get in the way of your good time."

Now you can look around and see how others guard their guilt. It's like having secret spy glasses. Once you've dealt with your own sense of guilt, you have an awareness of guilt in others. You see it in the way they cover their mouths when they talk, in the way their shoulders stoop when they walk, in their lack of eye contact. As you recognize these people, you're uniquely positioned to give them an important message.

What's that message? You're okay? You're forgiven? No. They'll need to get absolution from someone more important than you. Your message is this: "I'm guilty too." We're all guilty. You don't have to take on the role of judge or defender or savior ... just codefendant. It's not up to you to tell them how bad they've been or how good they can be. You don't need to sort out the rights and wrongs of their behavior. Just accept them as the same kind of good/bad human being that you are. "Sure, you've done things wrong. So have I. Let's play Pictionary." As you offer a nonjudgmental listening ear, they'll feel freer to open up.

They need your story. When you're in the midst of the crisis, you feel that you're the only one who has ever felt this way. Your loneliness is compounded by your sense of uniqueness. How could anyone else possibly understand?

But now you've been through it "and lived to tell about it." The telling is important. Your experience has given you valuable data about the recovery process, and people in the midst of the struggle need to know there's an endgame. So tell your story. You don't have to teach lessons, just say what happened to you.

In fact, you want to be careful about being too forceful with your story. Current strugglers might cling to the idea that their struggle is different from yours. Acknowledge that. You might say, "I'm not sure if this applies to your situation, but here's what happened to me." Let them draw their own conclusions, but give them the option of drawing hope and guidance from your experience. They can question whether your story applies to them, but they can't debate the facts of what happened to you. Put your story out there and let them process it.

They need sensible accountability. One of the worst things about the slippery slope is its uncertainty. You don't know whether you're heading up or down, and you have no idea how long this will take. Is that angry outburst a major setback or a minor slipup? When you're sliding around so much, it's hard to know where you stand.

But it helps to have someone checking up on you. If you know that someone is going to ask you how you're doing, you'll try extra hard to be doing well. That's the kind of accountability that's needed here—showing an interest in someone's progress.

In the latter stages of your own recovery, you can be holding others accountable. Be careful about this. You don't want to make them feel bad for their slipups; you know how slippery the slope is. But keep checking up on them. Give them an opportunity to motivate themselves.

There are two requirements for this job of holding strugglers accountable. You need to care, but you also need to know. You need to understand the process of recovery. Considering what you've been doing for the last few years, that shouldn't be a problem. But that's why we call it sensible accountability. There are tons of people who have no clue, and yet they try to hold people accountable. What's the matter with you? Still sulking? Why, it's been over a week! But you can bring the knowledge you've gained from your own painful experience. That will create sensible, sensitive accountability.

Look back over that list. What do strugglers need? Someone who's there, who listens, who humbly accepts them, who has a story to tell, who cares. That's you! They don't need preachers, motivational speakers, or dazzlers. They need what you have. We know it sounds corny, but the School of Hard Knocks has left you with a valuable diploma. You have hard-won knowledge and an important story to share.

Tips

So, where do you find these "others" to help? How do you put this final step into action? Here are a few ideas.

Institutionalize. Volunteer for established organizations such as churches and synagogues, the Y, community groups, charities, schools, prison ministries. Most of these have the helping operation already in place, and they can fit you right in. But make it clear that you're not just looking for an outlet for your creativity—you want to serve others. It's possible you won't get into people-helping right away, but the contacts you make in these organizations can eventually help you help others.

Look for the outcast. Whether you institutionalize or not, keep an eye out for the person who's cowering in the corner. At parties, find the people who aren't mingling. If you're sewing costumes for the school play, befriend the kid who's in the back row of the chorus, third from the left. The tide of society rolls right past these people. It's your job to counteract that.

Don't push yourself on others. Sadly, some people won't want what you're offering. Their loss. Don't get pushy about it. But also take care that you don't get too hurt by their rejection. Someone else will need your support. And maybe the same person who rejects you today will need you next week. (Remember that you were probably like that too, in the midst of your struggles.)

Be honest about your continuing struggles. Some helpers fall into a trap of hypocrisy: *How can I help anyone else if I don't have my own act together?* And so when they slip up, they hide it. They pretend to be perfect when they're not. If you do that, you're missing a great opportunity to model recovery for someone else. Strugglers don't need to see perfection. That will probably depress them. (*I'll never be that good.*) They need to see how people slip up and get back on track again.

Trust in invisible results. You won't always see the effect you have on people. You need to trust that you're making a difference. Tom travels around the country speaking at divorce-recovery and relationship-building seminars. Sometimes he'll return to a site the following year and hear people tell him how much they've grown. Sometimes he'll get a note from someone thanking him for inspiring a certain step forward. Those are wonderful pieces of feedback. But ninety percent of the time there's no such response. He has to trust that his words are bearing fruit in people's lives. If you push too hard to get visible results, then it's about you. You're not really giving freely; you're giving in order to get affirmation for yourself. Keep the focus on the person you're helping, and trust that good things are going on.

Our friend Deb is a fine example of this eighth ReStart step. When her husband left her a number of years ago, she was understandably a mess. Not only was she emotionally distraught, but her finances were messy too. She'd given up a great deal to support her husband's career, and now she was left virtually penniless. She had to work several jobs just to keep up with the bills and the rent on her small apartment.

With gritty determination and a supportive group of friends, she fought her way up that slippery slope. Emotionally she was growing stronger, but she was still struggling to make ends meet. She worked many hours as a piano teacher and as a receptionist in a doctor's office. Hard work for meager pay is always frustrating, but Deb was also dismayed by the dead-end quality of it all. Where was she headed? Was there any possibility for advancement? Would she always be sitting at a desk asking people to fill out forms?

Then she had an insight that changed her life. At that desk in the doctor's office, she was uniquely positioned to help people. The people who walked in and spoke with her were in pain. And not just physical pain. The doctors would tend to that, but these people usually had deep worries as well. Would they get over this injury? Would their insurance cover it? Would anyone care how they were feeling?

Too often, the forms that Deb was required to hand out just made things worse. People were reduced to policy numbers and medical data. Deb realized that they needed a human touch, and she decided that she could provide that. From that point on, this "dead-end" job became a calling. She did her best to calm and reassure the worried people who stood before her. Sometimes people even commented on how much her smile and pleasant words meant to them. She was completing her new start by helping others.

In the years since then, she's moved on to other jobs. But she has continued to help others wherever she has gone. In fact, she's helped us write this book, by researching and preparing the "real life stories" at the end of each chapter.

And that's our hope for you too — that you would move past acceptance and forgiveness and use your experiences to help others who need to start over.

REAL LIFE STORIES

→ CHRISTOPHER REEVE & JOAN

Christopher Reeve

In the spring of 1995, in a matter of a few seconds, Christopher Reeve's life changed forever. He had a terrible horseback riding accident, which left him paralyzed from the shoulders down and breathing with the help of a ventilator. You've probably heard of that tragedy, but you might not be aware of another life-changing event that took place years earlier, in 1992.

For many of us, marriage seems a simple, straightforward decision; but this was not the case for Christopher Reeve. His first long-term relationship was with Gae Exton, whom he met while shooting "Superman" in London. They lived together for almost ten years and had two children, but Christopher could never bring himself to make the commitment of marriage. He had grown up the product of a broken home and had gradually developed the idea that marriage was something of a sham. Everyone around him seemed to be in a troubled marriage, and he had no desire to join their ranks. Despite being happy with Gae and their children, he was restless in the relationship and happy to be away from home working. They finally parted under good terms with joint custody of the children, but Christopher was more convinced than ever that marriage was not for him.

In the summer of 1987 Christopher met Dana. They began dating, and he began to realize that his views of marriage would have to change. He was terrified, but agreed to go into therapy rather than lose Dana. As he worked through his fears, he realized that this marriage did not need to be like the ones he remembered from his childhood. The very act of commitment would make it stronger than his relationship with Gae had been. And so, five years after they met, Christopher and Dana were married.

Since Christopher's accident, he and Dana have worked

diligently to help others with spinal cord injuries. Christopher has written to every senator, advocating increased lifetime insurance caps and making follow-up calls on this issue. He's a speaker at various functions, encouraging increased research for such medical needs. He and Dana spend time answering letters from others with severe spinal cord injuries and do their best to encourage and give hope. Throughout all of this, they've found a remarkable thing happening in their own lives. The pain of their early relationship, when Christopher still thought that he couldn't get married, has faded. It's been replaced with a remarkable joy and closeness in their marriage as they reach out to help other people.

> *"I know I have to give when sometimes I really want to take."*
>
> —Christopher Reeve

Joan

A history of two nasty divorces could leave some people bitter and disillusioned about people and life in general. But that wasn't the case with Joan. Married young and divorced young, she worked her way through her own recovery with the help of her church and some friends, then decided to turn her energy toward helping others. She began helping out at divorce-recovery seminars sponsored by her church. She'd mind the book table, bring snacks, welcome participants, and do whatever she could to help the "walking wounded." The next year, she was asked to be a facilitator at the seminar, running one of the small groups. But she didn't feel quite ready for that kind of responsibility. For several years, as this seminar became an annual event, Joan continued to do other tasks. All the while, she was becoming known as a good listener. When people had problems, they knew they could call Joan. Her phone was constantly ringing with calls from friends and friends-of-friends who needed to talk.

As others sought her advice, Joan found herself feeling needed and whole. This didn't happen overnight, but it did happen, little by little. Eventually she felt confident enough to take on the responsibility of becoming a seminar facilitator and found it an extremely rewarding, although difficult, experience. After many years of a rewarding single life, Joan remarried and settled down to live happily-ever-after. But it didn't work out that way. Once again, Joan found herself going through a divorce and once again it was just plain awful. She went through a period of anger and depression. How could this be happening again? Especially when she had helped so many other people?

But after a normal, healthy period of grieving, Joan got back on track helping others. She let them know that they were not alone in their recovery and that their pain would not last forever. She's now embarking on a new adventure in helping others—as a foster parent.

NOTES

1. Lewis Smedes, *Forgive and Forget* (New York: Pocket Books, 1984), pp. 14-15.
2. This was cited without attribution in "Living with Furious Opposites," by Phillip Yancey, *Christianity Today,* September 4, 2000, pp. 70-81. That article was taken from Yancey's book *Reaching for the Invisible God* (Zondervan, 2000).
3. The Bible, James 1:2-4.

ABOUT THE AUTHORS

RANDY PETERSEN
& THOMAS WHITEMAN

RANDY PETERSEN has written numerous books, including several on psychological themes. He is coauthor of *Stress Test, Victim of Love?,* and *Angry with God* (all Piñon Press). As a freelance writer, Randy regularly creates educational curriculum for youth and adults, and has written articles for various magazines and Web sites. Randy is also an acting teacher, director, and actor in Philadelphia-area schools and theaters, with several original plays produced. He is the founding producer of the Encore Theater Company, which has developed and performed the original musical "Creating." A graduate of Wheaton College in Illinois, with a degree in ancient languages, he lives in Westville, New Jersey.

THOMAS A. WHITEMAN, Ph.D., is a licensed psychologist and the founder and president of Life Counseling Services. He has authored or coauthored several books including *The Marriage Mender* (NavPress), *Adult ADD, Victim of Love?* (both Piñon

Press), and *The Complete Stress Management Workbook* (Zondervan). Dr. Whiteman has interviewed with numerous radio and television stations across the country including WHUH in Washington, DC, and programs like "Mid-Day Connection" in Chicago, "On the Line" on WNYC in New York City, and "Minirith-Meier Clinic." He lives with his wife and children in Berwyn, Pennsylvania.

HERE'S HELP FOR GETTING YOUR RELATIONSHIPS BACK ON TRACK.

Victim of Love?

You know exactly what you want in a relationship but always end up with someone completely wrong for you. Examine unhealthy relationship patterns and learn to break the cycle.

Victim of Love? (Thomas A. Whiteman and Randy Petersen) $14

Stress Test

Develop a stress management plan to fit you! Through a short self-evaluation, *Stress Test* will help you discover which areas and patterns of your life need to be changed in order to reduce your "Stress Quotient."

Stress Test (Thomas A. Whiteman and Randy Petersen) $11

Get your copies today at your local bookstore, or call (800) 366-7788 and ask for offer **#6181**.

Prices subject to change.